𝒜 HISTORY & GUIDE
· to the ·
MONUMENTS
of
Chickamauga
National Military Park

A HISTORY & GUIDE
· *to the* ·
MONUMENTS
of
Chickamauga
National Military Park

STACY W. REAVES

Charleston · London

THE
History
PRESS

Published by The History Press
Charleston, SC 29403
www.historypress.net

First published 2013

Manufactured in the United States

ISBN 978.1.60949.986.0

Library of Congress CIP data applied for.

This is dedicated to veterans Staff Sargeant Chuck Webb USMC, Charlie Hanson, Max Melton and Colonel Robert Powell; and to the many other veterans I have known. Some have their stories in stone. Others are still waiting to have their stories told.

CONTENTS

ACKNOWLEDGEMENTS

This project has been an exciting one, but also challenging in many ways. I could not have completed this book without the assistance of many different people who were willing to do things at last moment and sometimes in a rush.

First, I must thank the staff of Chickamauga-Chattanooga National Military Park and Marie Paris with Eastern National Bookstore for this opportunity. Jim Ogden has been a wealth of information and of great assistance in finding sources and clarifying things. As the park historian, he is very busy, but he is always willing to offer me his time. Mr. Ogden is truly a great asset to the park and to the field of Civil War studies. I must also thank the other park rangers for marking maps, giving me directions and being pleasant to work with during my research visits. The librarians in the local history section of the Hamilton County Library are wonderful. They assisted me in finding sources and were more than willing to help me obtain copies of photos.

This project would not have been possible if it were not for the aid of the librarians and archivists at numerous archives and libraries. I must thank Sharon Avery at the Iowa State Historical Society for her assistance in locating sources and for photocopies. I must also thank the staff members at the University of Illinois Archives and the Abraham Lincoln Presidential Library and Museum who went to great lengths to find material on the Illinois monuments and commission. The archivists at the Minnesota, Connecticut and Massachusetts Historical Societies also receive my gratitude. I cannot thank Linda Chaffee of the Babcock-Smith Museum in Westerly, Rhode Island, enough. She assisted me in finding information, clarified many things about the workings of the granite industry and shared her own research with me.

The making of a book is a tedious process. I love to research, but I do not always welcome writing up the information. I cannot thank Janie Lampi enough for reading drafts of this book numerous times. She has been of great assistance in making sure that my tiredness and ignorance are not completely apparent. All the dumb mistakes a reader finds are totally mine. Lacking photography skills, I looked to Jane Beal for assistance. I am in deep gratitude to Jane for making several weekend trips to Chattanooga and photographing the monuments. I greatly appreciate the sacrifice that she and her family made on behalf of this project. Jane's work helps make the book more interesting and eye-catching. Some of the most important people involved in the completion of this project are Evelyn Rogers and the library staff at Tulsa Community College. They are wonderful, dedicated employees. I could not have completed this project without their valuable assistance.

Lastly, I cannot forget my family. My husband, George Reaves IV, gave me his encouragement and support throughout the entire process. He took over a great deal of the household chores and even read the rough drafts. I could not ask for a more wonderful spouse. Finally, my three daughters—Bessie, Camille and Claire—deserve special mention. They tolerated the not-so-great meals and forgetfulness during the last few weeks of writing and even hiked several miles of the battlefield over their spring break. I hope someday they will look back on that trip with fond memories.

INTRODUCTION

The hoary locks and bowed heads of many of you betoken that the weight of years is upon you and that in, the natural course of human events, soon the last survivor of these hard fought battles will be followed by patriotic citizens to the grave and this battle will remain only in recorded history.
—Humphrey D. Tate, private secretary to
Pennsylvania governor Robert E. Pattison

A few months ago, I was searching the Internet and ran across traveler reviews of historic sites. Several were Civil War battlefields. Most had great reviews of the battlefields and found them most interesting. One comment struck me, though. The reviewer commented that the park was great and that he really enjoyed the preserved battlefield. However, he was very disappointed with the number of monuments. It was not that there were not enough; rather, there were *too many*. The reviewer felt that the monuments spoiled his view of the battlefield and got in the way of preservation and understanding of the battle. Just the other day, a Civil War blogger asked whether battlefield monuments should be moved. I am saddened that people see the monuments as clutter and objects obstructing their view and understanding of the battle.

The soldiers began trying to honor their dead shortly after the battle. They would not forget the ultimate sacrifice given by so many. The Battle of Chickamauga left 34,624 men dead, wounded and missing. The battles for Chattanooga created 12,485 casualties. In December 1863, Major General George H. Thomas established the national cemetery in Chattanooga, and the Confederates, for practical purposes, started a cemetery in 1862. However, the southerners continued to use and provide maintanance for decades following the war. Even though these sites honor the dead and tell of the loss of life, they do not tell the entire story. They do not tell of the desperate attempts to hold a position, the horrific death of a battery commander or even of the attempts to save an army. The Union soldiers wanted future generations to know how much they willingly suffered, sacrificed and fought to save our nation. The aging veterans wanted to make sure that the Confederate soldier did not become a distant memory or completely forgotten.

Union veterans began the work of preserving the Gettysburg battlefield shortly after the war. They hoped to preserve the site so that they could tell the story of the grand battle and the Federal victory that changed the course of the war. Chickamauga would be different. Union veterans developed the idea of preserving the battlefield, but they wanted to honor and memorialize both sides. Both armies could claim victories. The South claimed a victory at Chickamauga, and the North claimed a victory at Chattanooga. The former soldiers realized that both sides fought hard for a cause that they believed at the time was right. Soldiers from both sides suffered and offered themselves for their respective cause. By preserving the site and honoring both armies, the veterans could physically express their feelings of reconciliation.

The military park would show that the nation had healed. It was not enough to preserve the land. The land did not tell the entire story. The veterans realized that they could communicate through the creation of monuments. The memorials marked their battle positions, showing how far they pushed and fought back. The stone and bronze monuments allowed the soldiers to tell their regiments' and states' stories of the fight and commitment to the cause.

Through the memorials, the soldiers could tell future generations of their courage and bravery. The states could honor their soldiers long after the last one died.

The veterans did not create the park for recreation. The men preserved the hallowed ground to tell of the bloody struggle for America. They wanted visitors to understand their fear and courage. The fields do not tell the story of the soldiers. The veterans tell the story through their monuments.

Part I

BATTLES OF CHICKAMAUGA
AND CHATTANOOGA

*The Chickamauga campaign will stand in the history of the war as
unequaled in its strategy by any other movement of the contest, and
as unsurpassed, and probably not equaled, for the stubbornness and
deadliness which marked the splendid fighting of the Unionist and Rebel
alike; and furthermore, it will stand as a substantial union victory.*
—*Park Historian Henry V. Boynton*

The Battles of Chickamauga and Chattanooga were instrumental
in sealing the fate of the Confederacy. Chattanooga, with its
railway lines and the Tennessee River flowing around it, became a
key city. The bustling little city that sat in the shadows of Lookout
Mountain provided a portal into Georgia and the lower South.

Early in 1863, Union forces defeated the Confederates near
Murfreesboro, and pushed the Rebel forces out of middle Tennessee.
Confederate general Braxton Bragg withdrew to the town of
Chattanooga. Bragg's retreat southward appeared disorganized, but
in reality, the commander hoped to give that impression as he dug in
and set up defensive positions in and around the city. Unfortunately,
Bragg's diligence failed him. In August, Union commander William
S. Rosecrans crossed the Tennessee River below Chattanooga and
forced the Confederates to retreat farther south. Now at LaFayette,

Georgia, the Confederate commander began building up his army. Reinforcements from east Tennessee, Mississippi and Virginia joined the Army of the Tennessee, thus creating a force of sixty-six thousand men. Realizing what the Confederates were doing, General Rosecrans began repositioning his men. By September 17, the Union general had formed a line from Jay's Mill down to Lee and Gordon's Mill. He now had his men within supporting distance of one another.

General Bragg devised a plan of action. This time, the Rebel commander planned to turn the Union left flank, drive the Federal forces back to McLemore's Cove and block the LaFayette-Rossville Road leading to Chattanooga. On the night of September 18, 1863, Bragg began positioning his troops for an attack. During the night, Confederate troops commenced crossing Chickamauga Creek and forming a battle line across from the Federal troops.

The following morning, Bragg began his attack. By 9:00 a.m., Confederate troops under Major General John B. Hood and Brigadier General Bushrod Johnson had moved toward Reed's bridge. Johnson, informed by locals that the enemy was in the area, shifted his columns into a battle formation. The Confederate general finally reached his destination at about 11:00 a.m. Waiting for him behind Pea Vine Creek were the Federal troops under the command of Colonel Robert H.G. Minty and mounted cavalry under John T. Wilder. Upon seeing the first elements of Johnson's men, the Union soldiers fired, and the battle began. By noon, Rosecrans had realized what Bragg was attempting and began shifting troops to strengthen his left flank.

While Minty tried to hold off the Confederates near Reed's Bridge, Major General William H.T. Walker's Confederate troops crossed Chickamauga Creek and began advancing toward the Union line. Back at Reed's bridge, Union troops moved back, allowing the Rebels to take the bridge. By midafternoon, the battle was raging along a three-mile stretch. Eventually, the Confederates pushed Rosecrans back to the LaFayette-Rossville Road, and the battle stopped for the night.

During the night, the Union army closed up its line and quickly threw up breastworks. Southern general James Longstreet arrived from Virginia with two more brigades to reinforce the Rebel army. Now with fresh men, Bragg began preparing for another offensive. The Confederate commander formed his army into two wings. General Leonidas Polk commanded the right side, and General Longstreet took command of the left. The Southern army was ready to begin fighting at dawn.

At sunrise, the Confederate troops advanced on the waiting Federals. At 9:30 a.m., Southern forces under John C. Breckinridge and Patrick Cleburne began forcing Union troops back. The Union breastworks slowed the short-lived advance. Rosecrans began shifting his troops to reinforce his left flank. As the general was busy shoring up his position, he received reports that there was a quarter-mile gap in the line. Quickly, Rosecrans moved a division to fill the space. The report was wrong. It had overlooked a Union division waiting in the woods. Now the Federals had created an opening in their line.

Confederate general Longstreet took advantage of the Northern army's mistake. He marched his men through the gap. The Union right flank broke down into chaos and fled toward Rossville, Georgia. Union major general George H. Thomas held on to what was left of the Federal extreme right. Eventually, Thomas, rallying the remnants of various Union divisions, formed a line on Snodgrass Hill. This stand earned him the nickname the "Rock of Chickamauga." Reserve commander Gordon Granger marched quickly to the sound of gunfire and helped Thomas stave off the Confederates' repeated attacks. By late evening, unable to hold any longer, Union troops withdrew and retreated to Chattanooga.

The intense fighting at Chickamauga left both armies appalled by their losses. Confederate casualties numbered almost twenty thousand. Union causalities numbered about sixteen thousand. Bragg had lost more than 30 percent of his effective fighting force and had ten generals killed or wounded. Sensing his loss in strength, the general did not pursue the Federal army and decided to try to starve the Northern army out of Chattanooga.

Bragg set up artillery and infantry on Lookout Mountain and along Missionary Ridge. The Confederates now had control of all supply routes to Chattanooga except over the Cumberland

Mountains. By mid-October, it looked as though the South might actually starve the Union soldiers out of Chattanooga. The Northern men had resorted to eating horses and forging for whatever they could find that was in the least bit edible. Determined to hold the city, Union commander General Ulysses S. Grant, who replaced Rosecrans, sent a successful mission to open a supply route. The Federal soldiers called it the "cracker line." President Abraham Lincoln, realizing the vital importance of holding Chattanooga, sent reinforcements. By early November, General William T. Sherman and General Joseph Hooker, as well as troops from Culpepper, Virginia, arrived to strengthen the Federal army.

Stronger, the Union army began preparing to attack the Confederates. On November 23, Grant received word that the Rebels were withdrawing from their positions. Testing this report, Grant sent Thomas's troops to demonstrate in front of the Southern forces. The Battle for Chattanooga began in earnest. General Phil Sheridan and Brigadier General T.J. Woods attacked the Confederate forces located on Orchard Knob, forcing the Southerners to abandon their position and move back to Lookout Mountain. The next day, Sherman attacked North Missionary Ridge. Meanwhile, General Hooker advanced against the Confederates holding Lookout Mountain. By noon, the Federal forces had joined up and reached a plateau on the mountain near the Craven family home. The Southern troops retreated up the mountainside to defensive positions. By 2:00 p.m., a heavy fog had enveloped the mountain, making visibility nearly impossible and forcing Hooker to stop the advancement.

The next morning, Generals Sherman and Hooker sent Northern forces forward against the Confederates, who had shifted all their forces to Missionary Ridge. Due to a delay, Hooker's men started their assault late. Grant sent Thomas's men forward from Orchard Knob to attack the Confederate center. Thomas's men, scaling the heights of the rugged ridge that rose from 200 to 500 feet, helped break the Southern line. Bragg began withdrawing his troops from Missionary Ridge and started retreating. Grant had won the city of Chattanooga and had opened the doorway for Federal troops to advance farther into the South.

Part II

THE GETTYSBURG OF THE WEST

Creating a National Military Park

It was the better of our nature that suggested the dedication of this park. It was the better angels of our nature that said, "here we will erect monuments, not to the victor alone, but to the victors and vanquished alike." It was the better of our nature that conceived this field of reconciliation.
—Senator Edward Stokes of New Jersey

It had been years since the gathered men had heard the roar of the cannons and felt the rush of adrenaline. They no longer wished for the excitement of battle. On this September day in 1889, the men's heads were beginning to gray, and wrinkles were appearing on their brows. They had gathered in Chattanooga, Tennessee, to reunite with their fellow veterans and to reminiscence about the late war.

The year before, Henry Van Ness Boynton and Ferdinand Van Derveer traveled to Chickamauga, Georgia, to visit the battlefield on which they had fought in 1863. During the battle, Boynton had served as a lieutenant colonel with the Thirty-fifth Ohio Infantry. A few months later, he fought in the Battle of Chattanooga, earning the Medal of Honor for his actions. Van Derveer served as a colonel in the same battle and regiment. The two men traveled across the battlefield, reminiscing about the horror and brutality of the war. As they toured the area, they found that the landscape had changed. They often found it difficult to find certain spots of importance. During this visit, the two men developed an idea to create a military park that would preserve the battlefield and honor those who served.

Excited, Boynton and Van Derveer presented their idea in Chicago in 1888 at the annual meeting of the Society of the Army of the Cumberland. The crowd of veterans thought it a great idea. The president of the society, former general William S. Rosecrans, a veteran of Chickamauga, appointed a committee to investigate the possibility and report back at the next annual meeting. Boynton used his position as a correspondent for the *Cincinnati Commercial Gazette* to promote the park concept. Union veterans had already begun marking positions at Gettysburg and preserving the battlefield. However, their efforts recognized only Union troops. Boynton wanted to make Chickamauga the "Gettysburg of the West," with one difference: the Chickamauga park would recognize and honor Northern and Southern soldiers. All the veterans loved this concept.

With enthusiasm, the committee met in Washington, D.C., on February 13, 1889, to begin the work of creating a park. Wanting southern support, the group postponed the meeting until select Confederate veterans could attend. The following day, the committee met again with War Department official Sanford C. Kellogg, also a veteran of the battle, and eight former Confederate officers. The group created the Chickamauga Memorial Association and compiled a list of influential men to whom they would extend an invitation for membership.

The association chose the anniversary of the battle, September 19, 1889, to hold its first official meeting in Chattanooga. This also coincided with the annual meeting of the Society of the Army of the Cumberland. Under a large tent, among the many speeches, the committee outlined its plans. The following day, the veterans gathered at a barbecue held at Crawfish Springs to elect officers for the Chickamauga Memorial Association. Demonstrating that it was truly a joint effort, the group elected former Northern generals John T. Wilder as president, former general Joseph Wheeler as vice-president, Joseph S. Fullerton as treasurer and

In 1889, the Army of the Cumberland gathered at Crawfish Springs for a reunion. During the event, the Chickamauga Battlefield Association organized and began creating the nation's first military park. *Courtesy of Hamilton County Library.*

Confederate brigadier general Marcus J. Wright as secretary. The association also included a board of directors made up of both former Union and Confederate soldiers. With full support of veterans organizations, the association began the work of creating the nation's first national military park.

Everyone agreed with Henry Boynton that the project needed government involvement. Sanford Kellogg, a member of the War Department, had already supported the idea and had even worked on mapping the battlefield several years earlier. Eager to make the park a reality, Boynton drafted a bill for introduction in Congress and enlisted the aid of Congressman Charles H. Grosvenor of Ohio to introduce it. The arguments presented for preserving the battlefield included not only preservation and commemoration but also military study. The park would not only be for the veterans but would also benefit future generations of military leaders. Fortunately, for Boynton and the committee, many Civil War veterans served in Congress and had fought in the battle. Congressional bill HR 6454 received the required support with few difficulties. On August 20, 1890, President Benjamin Harrison signed the bill into law. The

Civil War veterans now had a site commemorating their actions in the west, and the nation had its first national military park.

Boynton's bill included eleven sections. The park fell under the watchful guidance of the secretary of war, and its development and daily administration fell to the guidance of a three-person commission. The secretary of war appointed the commissioners. Two would be civilian, and one would be from the War Department. To guarantee Confederate representation, one commissioner had to be a southerner. The secretary of war appointed three veterans who had served at Chickamauga and Chattanooga. Joseph S. Fullerton of Missouri and Captain Sanford C. Kellogg both served in the Federal army, and General Alexander P. Stewart had commanded a Confederate division during the battle. Fullerton served as the commission's chairperson and resided in Washington, D.C. From there, he could negotiate any needed politics. Kellogg, an active-duty officer, served as the commission secretary. Alexander P. Stewart lived in Chattanooga and took on the task of supervising the everyday operations. The secretary of war appointed Henry V. Boynton as commission historian and secretary. To oversee park construction, the commission employed Edward E. Betts and Atwell Thompson as park engineers.

With the administration set in place, the task of creating the park began. The first step required the acquisition of the land. The bill called for preserving 7,600 acres of the battlefield. After the battle, many of the landowners returned and continued farming. A few sold parcels of their land, and new residents had since moved into the area. The park commission worked with more than two hundred landowners to negotiate the purchase of the various pieces of property that would eventually make up the park. It was not an easy task. Park commissioners often had to aggressively negotiate prices and, in some cases, condemn the land. By 1895, the commission had managed to acquire 6,527 acres. Now the work of restoration demanded their attention.

Several years earlier, Boynton and Van Derveer recalled how they struggled to recognize the land where they had once fought. Farmers had cleared woods and plowed new fields. Some fields had returned to the woods. Old roads had closed and grown over.

Residents had opened new roads and bridges. The establishing bill called for the land to appear as it had in 1863. The engineers surveyed the entire battlefield and marked off edges of fields. Engineer Thompson studied the roads, reopening the ones determined to be period correct and closing those opened after the battle. In the wooded areas, dense underbrush had grown up. Park employees began clearing this, returning the wooded areas to their battle appearance. By 1895, Thompson, Betts and the park employees had opened forty-one miles of road and cleared 3,500 acres of underbrush. This was in addition to restoring the wood lines. In just a few short years, the park commission had nearly returned the land to its battlefield appearance.

As park historian, Henry Boynton had the honorable but difficult task of marking battle lines and writing the official history. The historian consulted reports, maps and veterans' recollections. He also used the *Official Records of the War of the Rebellion* as it became available. The commissioners used reports held by private individuals and Confederate records. After careful study of the collected materials, Boynton worked with state commissions to mark the battle lines. Tablets representing each unit marked battlefield positions. Pyramids of cannonballs marked the sites where mortally wounded generals fell in battle, as well as the headquarters of each commander. To aid in the study of the battlefield, the commission erected five large observation towers. In 1893, the public's eagerness to view the park prompted the publishing of a guide and the commission also created a visitors' center at the Crawfish Springs Hotel.

The enabling legislation called for the park to commemorate the battle and encouraged states to erect monuments on the battlefield. In December 1893, the commission established guidelines for the erection of monuments, thus ensuring uniformity. To erect monuments to their troops, state commissions submitted their proposals to the secretary of war for acceptance. The proposals included the design along with its dimensions, weight and inscriptions. The inscriptions were limited to information on the individual unit's roles in the 1863 battles. The commissioners reviewed the inscriptions to ensure that they pertained only to the

Two women touring the battlefield, circa 1900. *Courtesy of Hamilton County Library.*

battle and did not praise one side or state political beliefs. This could often be a difficult hurdle for states to pass. In 1894, Alexander P. Stewart complained to his fellow commissioners about the inscription on the proposed Massachusetts monument. He objected to the line, "[T]he union, it must and shall be preserved." Stewart, a former Confederate, argued that the inscription violated the regulations because it implied a motive and a political sentiment. The other commissioners must not have agreed because they had earlier approved it. The committee required that all memorials be of granite or some other comparable stone and bronze. This would ensure that they could withstand the rigor of the enviroment and time. Once the secretary of war had approved the proposals, the states received permits for erecting their monuments.

Veterans wasted no time in working with their state legislatures in forming committees to erect memorials on the battlefield park. By March 1894, twenty-two different states were working on monument plans. Because it had no state affiliation, the park commission erected memorials for the Regular Army. With money provided by the federal government, the commissioners erected nine monuments to United States cavalry, infantry and artillery units. By late 1894, the park was beginning to appear as Boynton and the veterans had envisioned it. Tablets marking 212 units and 286 locations and distances, as well as fifty-one battery tablets, dotted the fields. The erection of state monuments had begun, and some were completed. It was time for the commissioners to begin planning the dedication of the nation's first military park.

With great anticipation, Congress appropriated money for the dedication. Commissioners worked tirelessly to prepare the ceremonies planned for the thirty-second anniversary of the battle, September 18–20, 1895. Chattanooga had a lot of work to do to prepare for the large gathering of veterans and families that would converge on the city. Mayor George W. Ochs, a Civil War veteran, formed committees and asked civic organizations to assist in preparing for the event. Realizing that there would not be enough rooms for the anticipated crowd, the mayor arranged for a civic organization to coordinate the boarding of visitors in private homes. In addition, a large tent built by the city offered lodging. To guarantee that all points of interest were accessible to the visitors, Ochs encouraged the two rail lines in the city to cooperatively run trains in a loop out to the battlefield. The Lookout Mountain train ran every two hours, and the street railroad line ran every seven minutes. The Tennessee River Transport Company provided river transport to the site of Sherman's crossing and to the mouth of the North Chickamauga Creek. Businesses throughout the city decorated the streets with bunting and decorations. The park commissioners commemorated the occasion with a multitude of speakers, bands and a parade.

September 18, 1895, dawned to the sun's rays bouncing off the highly polished granite of the state monuments that awaited the throngs of veterans to dedicate them to the memory of their fallen comrades. At nine o'clock in the morning, Michigan veterans gathered around their recently completed monument on Snodgrass Hill for their ceremonies. A few hours later, the veterans of Missouri and Wisconsin admired their state monuments and listened with rapt attention to the speeches presented. The activities continued into the afternoon. Men from Massachusetts, Illinois and Minnesota admired their monuments during the afternoon ceremonies. The old soldiers and their families listened intently to the speeches of now famous men such as General Lew Wallace of Indiana and Governor William McKinley of Ohio. After a full day of state activities, almost ten thousand veterans gathered that evening at the Society of the Army of the Cumberland's reunion in Chattanooga. Again, many of the famous generals gave speeches and congratulated the veterans and the commission on their hard work. Although it had been a busy day, it was only the beginning of the festivities.

The next morning, as the birds sang into the clear blue Georgia skies, almost fifty thousand people traveled the new battlefield to Snodgrass Hill. The two thousand seats set up by the commission quickly filled up, and the rest of the crowd remained standing or seated on the ground as an artillery battery and infantry regiment opened the ceremonies with a drill. At noon, a forty-four-gun salute brought everyone's attention to the speaker's stand. Vice President Adlai Stevenson began the round of dedication speeches. Generals from both sides of the battle entranced the audience with their presentations recalling the battle and the need for remembrance and reunion. Finally, a band roused the audience with patriotic pride.

On the evening of the second day, many attendees took the opportunity to reunite with old friends. Both the Army of the Tennessee and the Confederate Army of Tennessee held reunions in Chattanooga. Former generals addressed the crowds, and old soldiers swapped war stories well into the night. The next day held the opportunity to reminiscence more as they continued to dedicate the Chattanooga battlefield.

Eager to see the battlefield, the crowds swarmed Missionary Ridge and Orchard Knob in great anticipation. A cool fall breeze rustled the leaves as spectators watched a parade of Regular Army units, an artillery unit and the Civil War veterans march to the dedication site. Once again, a forty-four-gun salute opened the ceremonies and former generals from the battle gave speeches befitting the occasion.

After the dedication ceremonies, the commission continued to develop the park and educate visitors. States continued to build monuments on the battlefield. The park gave soldiers a venue to tell their story, smooth over the hurt feelings of war and remember

Gathering at Chickamauga and Chattanooga National Military Park, circa 1900. In the early years, veterans gathered on the battlefield for reunions and dedication of monuments. *Courtesy of Hamilton County Library.*

their heroes, ultimately continuing the healing process. George W. Ochs summed up the feelings of the veterans in his address by stating, "This park is the symbol of the nation's second birth, the holy ground where amity and reconcile have erected in granite and bronze the record of a country's heroes."

Part III

UNION MONUMENTS

Here sleep the blue. There sleep the gray. Here then we will raise memorials to both. There every state shall meet and do honor to its dead.
—*Senator Edward C. Stokes of New Jersey*

The late nineteenth and early twentieth centuries became an era of monuments. Before the Civil War, monuments in public spaces were few in number, and most were for military commanders or national leaders. The post–Civil War era changed the landscape. The interest and push by Civil War veterans to tell their stories created a surge in monument construction. The need to honor those who served and those who died in service spawned a drive in small-town communities to erect memorials. Veterans pushed to preserve the battlefields and erect memorials to honor the common soldiers and provide lasting records of their deeds.

At the start the twentieth century, monument companies flourished from quickly meeting the rising demands. Catalogues and magazines published by the United Daughters of the Confederacy and veteran organizations all carried advertisements. Readily available stock design monuments allowed organizations that were unable to afford a professional sculptor or the services of an artist to erect memorials inexpensively. The granite statue of the watchful soldier at parade rest or at attention became popular due to advertising, pricing and availability. The creation of the military parks provided a lucrative business for granite companies, enough that companies made extra efforts to edge out competition. In 1915, while bidding on work solicited by the Ohio Commission, the Van Amringe Company tried to gain an advantage over its competitors by arranging for the park engineer, Edward Betts, to affiliate himself with the company. Van Amringe informed the park superintendent that Mr. Betts was to "confine his service, and exercise his past experience and judgment exclusively in our behalf...and not in behalf of the other competitors, our rivals." The company hoped to use Betts's knowledge and familiarity to give it an edge in winning the bid. Unfortunately, the tactic did not work. The Ohio Commission selected the P.E. Bunnell Company of Cleveland, Ohio, instead.

Granite companies kept sculptors and stonecutters in their employ. Skilled workers were required to create the beautiful granite monuments. This often meant employing recent immigrants from Italy, Ireland, Germany and Scotland who had worked in the industry in their homeland and required little training. Skilled artisans brought their talent and knowledge to the granite companies, giving them the competitive edge. The businesses created drawings of proposed designs for potential customers or state commissions. Monuments requiring a sculpture required one of the company artists to sketch a design and then create a model in soft clay. Most often, this was life size or to scale.

From the model, the sculptor created a mold and made a plaster cast of the statue. The piece then went to the stonecutter. Laying the plaster cast next to the piece of granite, the cutter used a pointing tool to mark dimensions on the stone. The stonecutter repeated the process several times. After the large parts of the statue were finished, the stonecutter used his artistic eye to carve out the fine details of faces and other parts. Once completed, he set the statue upright for final inspection. Most customers chose designs from a selection of models—hence the common image of the soldier at parade rest. For an exclusive piece, the company or artist broke the mold, preventing duplication. Granite companies usually did not place the name of the sculptor or stonecutter on the monuments.

Stonecutters at Smith Granite Company in Westerly, Rhode Island. Notice the pointing tool for measuring the dimensions to transfer the design from the model to the stone. *Courtesy of Babcock-Smith House, Westerly Rhode Island.*

Some theorize that because a community of workers created the pieces, the company did not allow the artists to sign the monument. Sadly, the names of these talented artists are lost to time.

The push for memorializing and preserving Civil War battlefields coincided with a renaissance in American art and architecture. Inspired by the celebration of American industrialism and history at the Philadelphia Exposition in 1876, artists and architects began creating buildings and sculptures in a Neoclassical style. Their work celebrated American nationalism, idealism and nature. By the mid-nineteenth century, American artists and writers traveled to Europe to study. The École Nationale Supérieure des Beaux-Arts in Paris became the desired school for art training. As a result, the school influenced an entire generation of American artists. Those who were not fortunate enough to study in France or other European countries trained under master sculptors who had. In 1882, America boasted thirty-nine art schools, fourteen university art schools and fifteen decorative societies. At these schools, artists spent much time studying the human form; thus, the human form took center stage in their creations. Many of the newly created art institutions and societies often held expositions, allowing the artists to display their art (as well as advertise their services) and permitting the public to see their creations and talent.

The renaissance in American art provided veteran groups and others with a large number of sculptors to hire. The Beaux Arts and Neoclassical styles that became popular lent themselves to the form the veterans desired. These styles allowed the soldiers to tell the stories of the war, the sacrifices of the men and the gratefulness of the nation. Often, they allowed them to express their feelings of reconciliation. Because the American art renaissance and push for memorials intersected at the same period in history, many of the Civil War monuments found at Chickamauga and Chattanooga and at numerous other battlefields reflect this artistic style.

Minnesota

All hail and honor to Minnesota, all hail and honor to the Second Regiment for its valor and bravery at Chickamauga! May this monument stand in the sunny South forever, as enduring as the stars and stripes of our union.
—J.I. Egan at dedication of the Second Minnesota Monument

Their excitement could hardly be contained. The forty veterans and their families had traveled many miles for this day. Now in the bright sunlight, they stood in anticipation of the dedication of the Chickamauga-Chattanooga National Military Park. More importantly, this crowd, their hearts swelled with pride, gathered to dedicate a monument to the Second Regiment of Minnesota Veteran Volunteers and the Second Minnesota Light Artillery Battery.

The National Park Commission sent out an invitation for every state with troops involved in the Battles of Chickamauga and

Second Minnesota Volunteer regimental monument by Lorado Taft. *Photo by Jane D. Beal.*

Chattanooga to form commissions with the purpose of locating troop battle positions and to erect monuments on the park. Minnesotans quickly answered the call. Despite having a small number of men engaged in the battles, the governor of Minnesota was one of the first to appoint a commission. It was also the first state to complete the erection of monuments in the new park.

The State of Minnesota organized troops for the war effort shortly after the nation entered the conflict. In June 1861, the Second Minnesota infantry mustered into service at Fort Snelling, Minnesota. As part of the Army of the Ohio, both units found themselves traveling south to Kentucky and then on to middle Tennessee. In March 1862, the Second Minnesota infantry and artillery battery went with the Army of the Ohio to join General Ulysses S. Grant's army on the Tennessee River near Pittsburg Landing. By the time the men arrived, Grant had fought and won a fierce battle. The men found themselves detailed to burial duty. The Minnesotans participated in the siege of Corinth, Mississippi, and marched back north to Tennessee and Kentucky. There they fought to clear the Confederate forces out of middle Tennessee. At the Battle of Chickamauga, the Second Minnesota infantry fought the advancing Confederates during the opening of the battle. After repulsing four separate attacks, the regiment lost eight men and had forty-one wounded. Later in November 1863, the fighting to overtake Missionary Ridge left one-fifth of the Minnesota troops killed or wounded. Six Minnesota color guards gave their lives in defense of their flag during the battle.

The State of Minnesota would not pass up a chance to honor the valor and sacrifice of its Civil War veterans. In April 1893, the state legislature passed an act to allow the governor to appoint a committee to mark the battle locations of Minnesota troops at Chickamauga and Chattanooga. The act also called for the committee to erect suitable monuments to honor the state's soldiers. The governor wasted no time in appointing a commission. On May 27, 1893, in St. Paul, Minnesota, the newly appointed commissioners met for the first time. They elected former colonel Judson W. Bishop as president and W.A. Spaulding as secretary. Bishop seemed like a natural choice to lead the commission. He had served as an officer, leading the Minnesota troops during the battles. Spaulding had served with the Second Artillery Battery. With the formalities and organization of the group out of the way, they decided to send out invitations to granite companies for monument proposals.

The two men hoped to have the monuments completed and ready for dedication at the thirty-first anniversary of the battle in September 1894. The dedication would bring together the survivors of the regiment for the first time in many years. In June 1893, the commissioners met a second time to review the various design submissions. They needed to find monument designs that best honored their soldiers and that stayed within the $15,000 budget. George H. Mitchell of Chicago, a granite monument manufacturer, presented his design proposal to the committee during the meeting. All the designs submitted looked promising. However, the committee needed to see the battlefield first. The group traveled to Georgia to meet with the national committee and to review all of Minnesota's troop positions. After their trip to the battlefield, the commissioners selected George H. Mitchell to design two monuments to the Second Minnesota infantry and selected the J.M. Sullivan Company to create three monuments—including a monument to the Second Minnesota Artillery Battery.

One of the George H. Mitchell Company designs called for a bronze figure. Mitchell contracted with Chicago sculptor Lorado Taft to create the design. Taft, an instructor and the head of the sculptures department at the Chicago Art Institute, took on the project. Born in 1860 in Elmwood, Illinois, to a professor of geology at the University of Illinois, Taft became well educated. Unlike many artists of his day, he obtained a bachelor's degree and a master's degree from the University of Illinois before leaving to study in France. During the early 1880s, Taft studied at the demanding and famous École des Beaux-Arts in Paris for three years. He returned to the United States and opened a studio in Chicago. By 1886, art professionals and consumers had begun to notice his skills, and Taft received an invitation to become an instructor and the head of the sculpture department at the famed Chicago Institute of Art. The artist then spent his time not only creating his own works but also teaching the popular Beaux Arts style to students. By the 1890s,

Above, left: Artist Lorado Taft with a one of his busts, March 1887. *Courtesy of University of Illinois Archives.*

Above, right: Model of the bronze figures for the Second Minnesota Volunteer regimental monument. *Courtesy of Minnesota Historical Society.*

Taft's lectures were so popular that he was constantly in demand as a speaker on public art.

Much of Taft's work in the 1890s consisted of portrait busts and soldier memorials—not really what the creative and talented artist hoped to be producing on commission. For the Second Minnesota Infantry monument, Taft sketched a design that portrayed three soldiers. The center figure carried the American flag high over a soldier on his right, who clutched at a wound in his chest. The figure on the opposite side kneeled with his gun ready to defend the flag bearer and their wounded comrade. The sculpture, titled *In Defense of the Flag*, appropriately memorialized the actions and sacrifices of the Minnesota troops during the Battle of Chickamauga. Busy with lecturing and teaching classes, Taft left the actual work of

Faces of the color bearer and soldier on the Second Minnesota Volunteer regimental monument.

sculpting the design to one of his workers and therefore did not sign the piece.

By early 1900, Taft had begun taking commissions for larger pieces. Many were sculptures to help create civic beauty in Chicago and other cities. In 1903, the artist published the book *A History of American Sculpture*. It was an instant success. It was the first book to chronicle the development of American sculptural art. Schools across the country adopted it, and Taft's fame continued to garner him commissions. Around this same period, the City of Jackson, Michigan, decided to honor its Civil War veterans with a monument. The city contracted with the Van Amringe Company for a monument and requested the bronze figure from the Second Minnesota monument. Taft had destroyed the mold for the Chickamauga monument but offered to sculpt the city a very similar figure. This time, he enlarged the sculpture and made some minor variations in the design. Despite the beauty in his work, later in life, Taft believed that his early pieces, which included the Chickamauga monument, were some of his most hideous works.

With the monuments set in place, the Minnesota Commission had only to plan a dedication ceremony. The commissioners decided to offer a chance for the veterans to hold a reunion for

Dedication of the Second Minnesota Volunteer Infantry, September 18, 1895. *Courtesy of Minnesota Historical Society.*

their unit during the dedication of the Chickamauga Park. The men and their families would be able to visit with one another, other survivors of the battle and their former enemy, as well as participate in the dedication of the park. Forty veterans and their families, along with some Ohio veterans, gathered around the Second Minnesota monument on Snodgrass Hill on September 18, 1895. The Minnesotans listened to the representative of the state governor, former commanders and the park commissioners recount the heroism of the Minnesotans in battle and honor them with five monuments on the battlefield. After the speeches and fanfare, the group walked around the monuments and remembered the sacrifices made so long ago.

Massachusetts and Connecticut

We shall all hold an everlasting remembrance and gratitude for the mighty work they did to secure to us liberty and union in a country which shall remain one and inseparable now and forever.
—*Massachusetts governor Fred T. Greenhalge*

The men and their wives walked slowly across the hill to the large gray rectangular monument. It was a small group that was gathered around the monument, but the men were proud of their service. Only the Second Massachusetts and the Thirty-third Massachusetts Infantry served at the Battle of Chattanooga, but the members of these regiments would not let future Americans forget their contributions.

The state legislature first appropriated money to honor troops during the Civil War in 1883. The veterans used the money to erect monuments on the Gettysburg battlefield. Massachusetts was the first state to mark a battlefield and pay for the monument. Having already erected a monument at one battlefield, the state quickly acted to appropriate money to honor those who served on the western battlefield of Chattanooga. Massachusetts appropriated $5,000 for a monument, and the governor appointed a commission.

Massachusetts state monument on
Orchard Knob. *Photo by Jane D. Beal.*

Design selection took little time. John A. Fox, a noted architect in Boston, submitted a simple design. It seemed appropriate, especially since Fox had served in the battle. A member of a long and well-established Boston family, Fox joined the Massachusetts Second Volunteer Infantry in 1861. While serving with Company I, he fought at Chattanooga and followed William Sherman in his March to the Sea. Fox mustered out of service in 1865 and returned to Boston. Trained in architecture, he quickly opened his own office. Fox's talent and work led him to become a member of the Boston Society of Architects and the founder of the Boston chapter of the American Society of Architects. Perhaps some of his most important works were his monuments rather than his buildings. Not only did the former soldier design the Orchard Knob monument at Chattanooga, but he also designed one of the Massachusetts monuments at Gettysburg.

Like many other states, Massachusetts set aside money for the veterans to attend the dedication. Governor Fred T. Greenhalge, along with the lieutenant governor and other members of their staff, traveled by train to Chattanooga. The veterans joined the governor and his staff on the trip. The old soldiers arrived early enough to participate in the park dedication and then hold their own dedication ceremony on September 20, 1895. After the governor of Massachusetts dedicated the monument, the entourage enjoyed touring the battlefield before leaving the next day.

Connecticut state monument at Orchard Knob. *Photo by Jane D. Beal.*

Connecticut began making plans to erect a monument to its soldiers during the summer of 1895. The governor, acting on the General Assembly's bill, appointed a commission. Because the state only had two regiments engaged in the Battle of Chattanooga, only two veterans received appointments, Warren W. Packer and Captain Sanford E. Chaffee. Packer served with the Fifth Infantry. In January 1863, he became the commander for the regiment, leading it at Gettysburg and Chattanooga. Sanford served with the Twentieth Infantry. He enlisted in 1861 with his father and a brother. The young Sanford recruited a company of 140 men for the Twentieth and became its captain. Wounded at Gettysburg, the captain recuperated at a Baltimore hospital and returned to his men in time to join Hooker in the west. At the Battle of Chattanooga, Sanford received wounds that forced him to resign. The governor of Connecticut appointed him as a recruiter for the state for the remainder of the war.

The state legislature gave the Connecticut commissioners $2,000 for a monument on the Chattanooga battlefield. In order to select the best site for the memorials, the two men visited the battlefield during the park dedication in September 1895. They selected a site on Orchard Knob. In 1897, the men contracted with the Stephen Maslen Corporation of Hartford for a monument. Unfortunately, the cost of the memorial left no money for a dedication ceremony.

The State of Connecticut would not appropriate money for a dedication until June 1903. With money to spend for a proper ceremony, the two commissioners set the dedication date for October 15, 1904. Just as the men readied for the big day, the train carrying the state foot guard band for the ceremony crashed and delayed the guards. The commission rescheduled for the following day. The state governor held a grand reception at the Chattanooga auditorium. The foot guard band provided lively and appropriate music to set the mood. After the opening reception, the guards, in full grenadier uniforms, led the crowd in a march to the Read House to board carriages and travel to Orchard Knob. After waiting for the guard, whose members marched in ankle-deep mud for three miles, the ceremonies began. The band played "America," and the ladies put flowers at the base of the monument. The governor and other officials gave speeches honoring their soldiers. The following day, the Connecticut Commission and veterans returned north.

New Jersey

The hundreds of monuments, Union and Confederate standing side by side on these fields, are tongues that will ever tell of the unsurpassed courage and heroism of the American soldier.
   —Joseph S. Fullerton at the New Jersey dedication

It had been years since the former lieutenant had walked the battlefield. As he crossed the fields and woods, looking out over the valley below Missionary Ridge, he could not help but remember the wound he received while leading his men in battle along that steep mountain in November 1863. Now the former soldier retraced his steps along with Francis Child, another member of the New Jersey Commission. Both men were eager to see a monument raised somewhere on the Chattanooga battlefield in honor of the men who had fought so valiantly there.

After the park commission requested states to mark the battlefield, the State of New Jersey acted quickly to mark the positions of its troops. The Thirteenth and the Thirty-third New Jersey Infantry fought in the Battle of Chattanooga. They arrived with Major General Oliver O. Howard as part of Grant's reinforcements. The men of the Thirty-third, in their bright Zouve outfits, made for quite a sight for the weary troops in Chattanooga. Despite the doubts by their peers as to whether they could fight in the fancy clothing, the men proved to be formidable fighters at Orchard Knob and Missionary Ridge. More than one hundred New Jersey soldiers received wounds in the battle.

New Jersey holds the honor for being the first state to erect a state monument on the Chattanooga battlefield. The state legislature and the governor of New Jersey appointed a commission in 1894. The governor tasked two veterans, John J. Toffey and Francis Child, to mark the spots where New Jersey troops fought and to erect a state monument. Both men considered the appointment an honor, having served with the Thirty-third New Jersey. On the morning of November 23, 1863, as the battle began, Toffey was recovering from illness. Rather than miss the battle, he gathered his strength and led his company in the fighting on Missionary Ridge. While attempting to take the ridge, Toffey received a wound, and his heroic actions earned him the Congressional Medal of Honor. Interestingly, in April 1865, the lieutenant found himself an eyewitness to President Abraham Lincoln's murder and served as a witness in the trial of John Wilkes Booth and his co-conspirators. Child served with Company B of the Thirty-third New Jersey. After the war, the former soldier served as a circuit court judge in his home state.

The commissioners quickly located the battlefield positions and began making plans to erect markers. The New Jersey legislatures did not appropriate money for two regimental markers and a state monument until 1896. With $5,000 to spend, the commissioners

New Jersey state monument on Orchard Knob. *Photo by Jane D. Beal.*

quickly sent out invitations for designs and bids to all the major monument companies. The companies were more than happy to supply proposals. Toffey and Child received sixty different designs from seven of the largest firms in the nation. The men set a date to review the proposals and make a choice. On the review date, each company explained its various ideas but not the prices. To be certain that cost did not influence their choice, the commission placed the bids in envelopes numbered according to the designs. They selected their design and then opened the bids. On May 27, 1896, the commission selected designs by the Badger Brothers Company of West Quincy, Massachusetts, and awarded it a contract to construct the New Jersey monuments at Chattanooga.

As October ended, the New Jersey Commission, the legislature and the Civil War veterans of the state grew excited. Their monuments at Chattanooga were near completion. The graying men busied themselves with plans for the dedication ceremony. On November 1, 1896, the Badger Brothers Company reported that the markers and the state monument were complete. The commissioners finalized their arrangements for the dedication and chartered a special Pullman car for the New Jersey delegation to travel from Jersey City to Chattanooga. The entourage included a representative for the governor, the ex-president of the New Jersey Senate, the Speakers of the House and Assembly, members of the Grand Army of the Republic and survivors of the both regiments.

The group left Jersey City on November 20 and arrived the following day. The mayor and prominent citizens of Chattanooga welcomed them at the Read House that evening with a festive reception. The following day, the entourage visited the cemetery and the battlefields, recalling the scenes of the battles and the decisive decisions made. The group arose early on the twenty-third, ate breakfast and then took electric cars to the foot of Lookout Mountain. From there, they traveled on the recently installed incline railroad up to the top. After lunch, the New Jersey group traveled in seven landaus decorated in American flags and pulled by teams of gray horses. The carriages wound their way through the town to Orchard Knob for the dedication ceremony. The statue on top of the monument cast a shadow over the crowd as people took their seats. The flags and bunting decorating the memorial fluttered in the autumn air as the crowd listened to the state senator and other distinguished speakers praise the New Jersey veterans. The following day, the members of the delegation boarded the train and headed for home, taking pride in the work they had done to honor their veterans.

Michigan

The granite monuments are not more firm now than the men of Chickamauga.
—Captain Charles E. Belknap at Michigan Dedication

It had been years since most of the men had seen one another. Now they rode across the battlefield that they had once desperately fought across. The members of each unit gathered around their regimental monuments in remembrance. The Twenty-first Michigan listened to the speech presented by its former captain. He had been merely a boy during the battle. Michigan had lost 1,500 soldiers in the Chickamauga Campaign, and it would not forget their courage.

In February 1895, Michigan began the process of recognizing and memorializing its Civil War veterans. The state legislature appropriated $20,000 for a commission to erect monuments to the Michigan troops on the newly formed Chickamauga and Chattanooga National Military Park. The governor selected five veterans of the battle to serve as commissioners. Captain Charles E. Belknap took the position as chair of the commission and headed up the project. Belknap seemed like an excellent choice as chair. In 1862, the veteran enlisted in the Twenty-first Michigan at the age of fifteen. During the Battle of Chickamauga, the young man received four wounds. After the war, he busied himself with studying and writing Michigan's history. Because Belknap had served as a United States representative, he also had political ties. With the former captain in charge, the men set

Thirteenth Michigan Infantry regimental monument at Chickamauga. *Photo by Jane D. Beal.*

about in earnest to select appropriate designs to tell the story of the Michigan troops in the battle and to honor them.

With thirteen different units to recognize with a monument, the commission wasted no time in requesting design proposals. It immediately sent out circulars inviting design submissions by March 23, 1895. The commission hoped to have the monuments in place and ready to dedicate during the park ceremonies in September. When the committee met again in March, it was overwhelmed with the number of submissions. It had nearly six hundred designs to examine over four days, and the men found themselves in a quandary. Many of the proposed monuments were more suitable for a cemetery rather than a battlefield. Those that were truly battlefield monuments were beyond the commission's financial means. The five men had to select designs that were appropriate for the battlefield *and* met their budget. With much discussion, they selected proposals from three different companies. The Smith Granite Company of Westerly, Rhode Island, would create the monuments for the Second and Fourth Cavalry; Artillery Batteries B and D; and the Ninth, Eleventh and Thirteenth Infantries. Maurice Powers Company of New York would design the Tenth, Twenty-first and Twenty-second Infantry monument. It would also erect a monument to the engineers and mechanics. The Venerable Brothers Company would fulfill the contract for the Twenty-first Detached Infantry.

When September arrived, all the Michigan monuments were standing firm on the battlefield, awaiting dedication. The state commissioners and survivors of the battle traveled to Georgia for the dedication of the park. They spent the morning at Snodgrass Hill, participating in the park ceremonies. Afterward, they traveled across the battlefield to each Michigan monument for individual dedications. Members of the regiments and of the Michigan commission gave speeches at each memorial. After the ceremonies, the veterans held regimental reunions and shared stories of days past.

Ohio

*The wounds of war have been soothed and healed, but the
men who fought here on either side will be remembered for their
bravery and heroism—and the men who saved the union will
never be forgotten.*
     —*Governor William McKinley*

Ohio had offered and sacrificed many of its sons during the
Battles of Chickamauga and Chattanooga. Five officers from
Ohio commanded a division in the battle. Of the thirty-six
battalions engaged, Ohioans made up ten. Out of 158 regiments
fighting in the battle, Ohio offered 44. The state legislature had
no hesitation in honoring the state's heroes on the battlefield. It
erected fifty-five monuments to its units engaged in the battle
and two large state monuments.

On May 4, 1891, after the announcement of the creation of
the Chickamauga and Chattanooga National Military Park, the
Ohio General Assembly passed a bill calling for a commission
composed of Chickamauga veterans. Ohio's governor appointed
Generals John Beatty and Ferdinand Van Derveer to the
commission. Van Derveer had not only commanded troops
during the battle, but he had also helped to originate the idea
of a battlefield park. John Beatty's brigade had been one of the
first to cross Lookout Mountain during the battle. Charles H.
Grosvenor, a senator from Ohio, also received an appointment.
Grosvenor had introduced the bill for the park's creation to
Congress. Five other men, prominent in Ohio, agreed to serve
on the commission, too. These men marked the battlefield for
three cavalry units, ten artillery batteries and forty-two infantry
regiments. The state appropriated $95,000 for the monuments
and another $5,000 for the commission's expenses.

To begin their task, Van Derveer and the other state
commissioners decided to visit Chickamauga and Chattanooga. On
November 24, 1891, the men toured the battlefield and returned
the following September with forty-five veterans of the battle to
help them select suitable sites for the monuments. After their visit,

Eighth Ohio Infantry regimental monument at Chickamauga. *Photo by Jane D. Beal.*

the commission received approval for thirty sites as being historically correct. In May 1894, after some debates and reviewing battle reports, the secretary of war finally approved all fifty-five sites. While the commission studied the battle lines and tried to determine the historically correct locations of the Ohio troops, it also began working on erecting monuments. At their meeting in April 1893, the men made plans to get competitive bids by sending out an invitation to all the prominent granite companies. After receiving more than five hundred designs, the commission reviewed the submissions and then put them on display in the halls of the Ohio House of Representatives for the public to view.

With more than fifty-five monuments to erect on the battlefield, the commission would need to select numerous designs. To meet this need, the men selected proposals from six different granite companies. Smith Granite of Westerly, Rhode Island, received a contract to create monuments for fourteen infantry regiments and two artillery batteries. The commission contracted Vermont Granite Company of Barre, Vermont, to produce seven regimental monuments, one artillery battery and a monument to the Ohio sharpshooters. Thomas W. Fox, an architect in Cincinnati, signed a contract to create five regimental monuments. The commission also chose designs presented by Maurice J. Powers, a prominent owner of a New York bronze foundry. Powers would use his designs to create five monuments with bronze reliefs. E.F. Carr and Company of Quincy, Massachusetts, accepted contracts for eighteen monuments.

Two monuments would honor two cavalry regiments, and four would memorialize artillery batteries; the rest would be for infantry.

The commissioners agreed that all the monuments should have the state seal on them. The men hired famous Ohio sculptor Charles Niehaus to design the seal. Niehaus, born in 1885 in Ohio, began his early career carving wood and marble. As an aspiring young artist, he studied sculpting at the McMicken School of Design in Cincinnati, Ohio, and traveled to Europe to study at the Royal Academy in Munich, Germany, between 1877 and 1881. After completing his training in Neoclassical art in Europe, he returned to Ohio and opened a studio. His talent and training quickly helped him land a commission for a sculpture of the late president Grover Cleveland and for a piece in Statuary Hall in Washington, D.C. The artist again felt the need to further his training by studying in Europe and moved to Rome to study ancient sculpture. In 1885, he returned to the United States and opened up a studio in New York City. By the 1890s, Niehaus had become a noted and accomplished portrait sculptor. His talent landed him commissions

Artist Charles Niehaus works on a bust in his studio. Niehaus designed the state seal for the Ohio monuments. The artist is most famous for his works in Statuary Hall in Washington, D.C., and for the reliefs for the doors to the Library of Congress. *Courtesy of Archives of American Art, Washington, D.C.*

for seven more sculptures in Statuary Hall in Washington, and the relief on the doors to the Library of Congress. The work of creating the state seal for the Ohio Commission would be a small job.

Smith Granite Company, a well-established company, did not find the task of erecting sixteen monuments on the battlefield to be challenging. The company, founded in 1845, had a long and respected history of producing high-quality monuments. During the late nineteenth and early twentieth centuries, the company employed several talented sculptors and stonecutters. These men, many of them immigrants, created beautiful pieces of sculpture and details on the Chickamauga monuments. Sometimes as many as seven stonecutters labored to turn a large piece of granite into a piece of art that befitted the sacrifice of the soldiers it honored.

Large granite companies and foundries won most of the design contracts for the Ohio regimental monuments. An individual artist did have at least one of his designs selected by the veterans. Leopold Feitweiss received a contract for the Ninth Ohio infantry monument. Feitweiss, the son of a German immigrant, spent his life working in marble and stone. His father, Charles Feitweiss, owned a marble company and worked as a marble carver and sculptor. He taught his son these skills as a young man. By 1875, Leopold Feitweiss had learned all he could from his father and moved to Rome to further his study and skills. A year later, he returned to Ohio to take a position as an instructor of modeling at the Ohio Mechanics Institute. By 1894, Feitweiss's had earned membership in the prestigious Cincinnati Art Club.

The veterans of the various regiments often made the final selection of their monument. The members of the Sixth Ohio Volunteer Infantry settled on a design that cost $2,100. The state legislature appropriated only $1,500 for each monument. Determined to have their chosen monument, the veterans took subscriptions to raise the extra money to fund their monument. The E.F. Carr Company of Quincy, Massachusetts, had received the contract to erect the monument for the One Hundred Twenty-fifth Ohio Volunteer infantry. Instead of using one of Carr's designs, the veterans submitted a design created by Charles H. Clark. Clark, from Columbus, Ohio, had served throughout the war with the regiment. The unit, commanded by Colonel Emerson Opdycke, fought a hard, desperate battle at Snodgrass Hill during the

Tiger on the One Hundred Twenty-fifth Ohio Veteran Volunteer Infantry
monument on Snodgrass Hill, Chickamauga.

first day of fighting at Chickamauga. Known as "Opdycke's Tigers," Clark prominently incorporated the sculpture of a tiger on the monument. In honor of their commander, he also included a bas-relief of Opdycke and a bronze relief scene of the regiment in battle.

Amazingly, with so many monuments to erect and six different companies performing the work, all the Ohio monuments stood complete and ready for dedication by September 1894. The commission chose to dedicate its monuments the same weekend as the park dedication, thus joining several other states in ceremonies. This allowed the veterans to gather with their regiments and to dedicate the new park. On September 18, 1894, at 2:28 p.m., commission president General John Beatty opened the Ohio ceremony. The veterans listened to speeches recounting the actions of the Ohio units during the battle and proclamations in support of reconciliation. Ohio governor William McKinley gave a rousing speech that honored the men and the memory of the late war. After

Ohio monument on the
Ohio Reservation along
Missionary Ridge. *Photo
by Jane D. Beal.*

the ceremony, the veterans dispersed to gather with their former
comrades at their regimental memorials.

Despite erecting the regimental monuments, Ohio was not finished
honoring its soldiers. In 1902, the Ohio legislature appropriated
$30,000 to erect a state monument on Missionary Ridge in honor of
those serving in that battle. The Van Amringe Company accepted the
contract and quickly went to work. Using a design created by Leland
and Hull Monument Company of New York, the forty-five-foot-tall
monument featured not only a shaft but also four life-sized figures.
The commission hoped to dedicate the Missionary Ridge monument
on November 12, 1903. The massive size of the monument frustrated
the company, though, and led to delays. Van Amringe, like many of
the companies, subcontracted the hauling and movement of pieces
with locals. Using trains and wagons to cart the massive pieces up

the mountain, the work became slow and tedious. On October 3, 1903, park engineer Edward Betts reported that all the pieces of the Ohio monument were on the park grounds except for the two pieces forming the shaft. One remained on a rail car, and the other was at the junction of Dodd and McCallie Avenues en route to the ridge. The park commissioners reported a few days later that the dedication for the monument seemed delayed indefinitely. The smaller pieces of the shaft lay near the electric railroad, which was once again broken.

Learning that the pieces of granite were still not in place, William van Amringe visited Chattanooga in early October to investigate the cause of the delays. To his dismay, the companies hired to move the pieces did not have the proper equipment to haul such large stones. They attempted to build special trucks to move the granite and spent considerable time experimenting with their new rig. For days, pieces of the monument lay alongside the road, awaiting new rail engines to move them. To add to the complications, the derricks used for lifting the

Constructing the Ohio state monument on Missionary Ridge. Notice the obelisk on the ground waiting to be lifted into place. *Courtesy of Chickamauga and Chattanooga National Military Park.*

granite proved inadequate and needed reinforcement. On October 20, Van Amringe reported that he had finally received word that the first of the two stones were on top of the mountain. In March 1904, the park engineer reported that the workers had completed the Ohio monument on Missionary Ridge. Finally, on November 12, 1904, the Seventh U.S. Cavalry band opened the dedication ceremonies for the monument.

In March 1915, the State of Ohio prepared to dedicate the Ninety-seventh Ohio regimental monument on Missionary Ridge. While the veterans prepared for the dedication, the state legislature prepared to pass a bill to authorize a monument on Lookout Mountain. In June 1915, the bill appropriated $20,000 to erect a monument on the mountain and purchase land if necessary. After the state commission made its application to the park commission, the superintendent informed it that no state made it to the top of the mountain— therefore, states could not erect state monuments there. The New York monument at the top was a peace memorial and therefore not in conflict with park regulations.

The Ohio Commission settled with erecting its second state monument near the Craven House. Upon putting out bids, the Van Amringe Company jockeyed to receive the contract. It had already erected one Ohio monument and several others on the battlefield. It argued that the memorial on Missionary Ridge gave it the required experience needed to erect a large monument on the difficult mountain terrain, and it also secured the promise of engineer Betts's assistance. Perhaps the difficulties at Missionary Ridge worked against them. The commission awarded the contract to the P.E. Bunnell of Cleveland, Ohio. The Lookout Mountain design called for a large shaft with four panels along the base. Two panels contained inscriptions. The others featured low reliefs of a soldier at parade rest and a female figure of peace. An electric train ran up to Craven House. Taking advantage of this transportation, the commission added a series of concrete steps leading from the monument to the rail line about one hundred yards away.

The P.E. Bunnell Company set its men to work. The large pieces of granite arrived at the mountain unharmed and even made it to the site. The difficulty lay in erecting the monument. In October 1916, the company built a large derrick to lift the heavy stones into place. The

Above, left: Mold for the bronze panel for the Ohio monument on Lookout
Mountain. The relief depicts the image of "Peace." *Courtesy of Chickamauga and
Chattanooga National Military Park.*

Above, right: Ohio monument located near the Craven House on Lookout
Mountain. *Photo by Jane D. Beal.*

ninety-foot-high derrick proved too weak and broke. The workers set
about erecting a second derrick, and again, as they began to lift the heavy
stone, this one broke too. Fortunately, the stone remained unharmed.
The owner of the house next to the monument site became furious
about the massive derrick and granite that came crashing near his home.
Agitated, the homeowner complained to the park superintendent,
threatening to take out an injunction against the contractor. He argued
that the work endangered his home and threatened his life. The workers
remounted the derricks and strengthened them. In December 1916,
work halted again. This time, the weather caused a delay. It was too
cold for the concrete to set properly. Mr. Betts also halted the work as he
learned that Bunnell had unpaid accounts around town.

As the contractor struggled to erect the monument on the side of Lookout Mountain, the Ohio Commission began preparing for a dedication ceremony. The men agreed on Memorial Day 1917. As the troubles erecting the massive monument mounted, the commissioner moved the date to September 17, 1917. As early September arrived, the veterans eagerly looked forward to the ceremonies. However, when America entered World War I, the military made use of the Chickamauga battlefield. Troops set up camps in the area and practiced drilling. On September 7, the Ohio commissioners received word that they would have to delay their ceremony again. The trains in the area were committed to moving soldiers to southern posts for training, and there would be no room for the veterans. On October 17, 1917, the Ohio veterans took the trains to Chattanooga and rode the electric line to their monument on Lookout Mountain for dedication.

Landrum Monument

A lone monument in the shape of a cross stands in the woods not far from a pyramid of cannonballs. The cross does not mark the grave or death site of a general. Instead, it marks the site of a lieutenant who gave his life during the Battle of Chickamauga. The single cross tells the story of a family stricken with grief, as well as their attempt to memorialize their loved one.

Park regulations and the commission requested that states erect monuments. The guidelines said very little about families and individuals. During the late spring of 1894, the park commission received an application for a mortuary monument to Lieutenant George W. Landrum of the Second Ohio. The Landrum family submitted the application hoping to tell of his gallantry and to memorialize him. Their loved one, detached from his regiment, served special duty to Federal general George Thomas during the battle. At about four o'clock in the evening on September 20, General Thomas gave Landrum a message to deliver to General William S. Rosecrans. While delivering the message, a bullet struck the lieutenant and killed him. Just

Memorial for George W. Landrum. The lieutenant's family erected the cross on the site where he was mortally wounded. *Photo by Jane D. Beal.*

before dying, Landrum said, "I am glad to give my life in so glorious a cause."

The family asked to erect a private memorial to their beloved lieutenant near the spot where he fell. A man named Dr. Thompson, who saw Landrum shot from his horse during the battle and stayed with him until he died, spent two days searching for Landrum's grave and remembered distinctly where the young man fell. The family hoped to erect a twelve-foot-high granite cross on the spot. Landrum's brother-in-law, Obadiah Wilson, argued that Landrum was "a brave and gallant young officer, who fell while heroically endeavoring to convey a message."

The secretary of war approved the monument. This would be the first personal monument erected on the battlefield. The suggested inscriptions received approval, but the secretary of war required "erected by his family" to appear on the monument. He did not want to give people the impression that the State of Ohio or the park commission erected such a monument to one individual.

Kansas

How those who perished here, whose blood darkened these slopes, ravines, and hillsides, are revered by their people at home, is told in mute and silent language by the monumental spires that have been erected in this National Park.
—Illinois governor John P. Altgeld

During the 1850s, the debate over states' rights and slavery centered on Kansas. The fighting and raids on their cities gave Kansans an early taste of what the future would hold. Citizens of the territory lost lives and property over the controversial issue of slavery. When the South seceded and the war began, the people of this western state did not hesitate to enlist in the cause of the Union. The fighting often took the men to far places like Virginia and Georgia.

Despite the Chickamauga battlefield being far from Kansas, the state legislature quickly responded to the call to mark battle lines and erect monuments in the park. On February 18, 1895, Governor E.N. Morrill approved an act to create a state commission to erect monuments honoring Kansas's Civil War soldiers. The bill specified that the commission include five soldiers from the state who had served at the Battles of Chickamauga and Chattanooga. It also gave the men $5,000 to spend on monuments to the Eighth Kansas.

The men of the commission had personal ties to the battle and wished to see the Kansas troops honored. At least three of the five men appointed to the commission directly served in the Battles of Chickamauga and Chattanooga. At least two served in Kansas regiments. The governor appointed J.L. Abernathy of Leavenworth to the commission. In 1856, Abernathy migrated to Kansas and established the largest furniture factory west of the Mississippi River. In 1861, he enlisted in the Eighth Kansas, and the men quickly promoted him to captain of Company A. Abernathy left the army at the end of the war with the rank of lieutenant colonel. Another commissioner, Solomon R. Washer, did not immigrate to Kansas until 1860. Moving from Indiana, Washer settled in Atchison, where he became a grain merchant, postmaster and a member of the board of education. Washer enlisted in the Eighth Kansas as a private but quickly received promotion to sergeant major. During the Battle of Chickamauga, he received a wound. Despite the injury, Washer continued serving in the war and mustered out in 1866.

Eager to begin work, the Kanas commissioners met in April 1894 in order to mark battle lines and select appropriate locations for the monuments. While they visited the battlefield, the men also advertised for design proposals. After receiving several submissions, the commissioners received word that parties doing the work were to submit their designs to the Wisconsin Commission in Milwaukee. The commissioners decided to send two representatives to Milwaukee to review proposals and sign contracts. After looking over the submissions, the men selected three monuments. They would place one at Chickamauga, one at Orchard Knob and one on Missionary Ridge.

The commissioners contracted with Smith Granite of Westerly, Rhode Island, for the monuments and with American Bronze for the state seals. The Missionary Ridge monument marked the site

The bronze infantryman sculpture on the Eighth Kansas Monument along
Missionary Ridge.

where the Eighth Kansas broke through the Confederate lines along
the crest of the ridge. The monument featured a Barre granite base
with a bronze statue of a soldier. The memorial, overlooking the
city of Chattanooga, stood seventeen feet and eleven inches tall.
For the Orchard Knob location, the commissioners chose a simple

boulder design with a bronze panel. The Chickamauga monument remained simple in design as well. It featured a stone design with a bronze panel. Smith Granite Company completed the monuments in time for Kansas to dedicate its monuments at the park dedication on September 18, 1895.

Pennsylvania

Let us before these monuments, as before a shrine, mingle our tears and droop our flags and listen to the solemn dirge in memory of the patriotic dead, both North and South & let us again resolve that the men who fell on these fields, have not died in vain.
—*Pennsylvania governor Daniel Hastings*

The men of Pennsylvania climbed Lookout Mountain and stared at the large sheer walls of rock that stood between them and the enemy. The soldiers of the Keystone State pushed the Confederates from Orchard Knob and fought valiantly on the fields of Chickamauga. As gray crept into their beards and wrinkles developed along their brows, they felt the need to memorialize their actions on the battlefield. Future generations would not forget their heroism or sacrifice.

In the spring before the Chickamauga battlefield dedication ceremonies, the Pennsylvania state legislature passed a bill authorizing a state commission to mark battle lines and erect monuments. Although he was not a veteran, Governor Robert E. Pattison had great respect for the aging soldiers of Pennsylvania. He wasted no time in appointing a commission. The governor selected members from each regiment that served in the battle. This gave each unit a voice. In the Supreme Court room of the Pennsylvania Capitol, the aging veterans met to begin the task of remembering the great battles. Alexander W. Bergstresser of the Seventy-ninth Pennsylvania called the meeting to order, and the group quickly elected him temporary chair. Although representatives from each unit had received an appointment, they would only help establish

Monument to the Seventy-ninth Pennsylvania by Richard W. Bock. *Photo by Jane D. Beal.*

battle lines. A smaller group of commissioners took on the task of contracting the memorials and overseeing the dedication ceremonies.

The Pennsylvania legislature appropriated $25,000 to erect seventeen monuments on Lookout Mountain, Missionary Ridge and Orchard Knob, as well as on the Chickamauga battlefield. Wanting each unit to have its own unique memorial, the commission advertised for proposals and bids. After reviewing the numerous submissions, it awarded contracts to Badger Brothers Company, Maurice Powers Foundry, Smith Granite Company and George H. Mitchell, who submitted a design by sculptor Richard W. Bock. It is likely that representatives of each regiment selected the design for their monuments.

Because the commissioners selected individual designs, most of the seventeen monuments are unique. Knapp's Battery D selected a monument created by Sylvester W. McCluskey, a member of the regiment and a member of the Pennsylvania Commission. In July 1861, Joseph M. Knapp, serving as a first lieutenant with the Twenty-eighth Regiment, received authority to begin recruiting a battery. Looking for young men eager to serve, Knapp traveled to Pittsburgh to recruit. Upon arrival, he found Charles A. Atwell and James D. McGill busy forming a regiment. The two men offered Knapp an artillery battery. Knapp's battery served in the Battles of Cedar Mountain and Gettysburg. After the Battle of Chattanooga, they followed General William T. Sherman in his March to the

Sea and participated in General Joseph Johnston's surrender at the end of the war. The battery fought a hard-won battle on Orchard Knob during the Battle of Chattanooga. Sylvester W. McCluskey served with the battery as a second lieutenant. McCluskey's design featured a cannon similar to one the battery used in combat, with an American flag loosely draped over it. The front featured the years of service. The lieutenant's design represented the battery and honored its years of service.

The members of the Seventy-ninth Pennsylvania decided to raise additional funds to erect the monument design that they chose. The regiment, composed of men mostly from Lancaster County, Pennsylvania, held the ground near the Kelly Farm from Sunday morning until evening during the Battle of Chickamauga. Remembering the hard fight and the losses, the veterans chose an allegorical design. The bronze figure featured a color sergeant falling. Just as the sergeant falls, another soldier catches the flag and holds it high, thus preventing it from falling to the earth and keeping it to the front of the battle. Chicago artist Richard W. Bock submitted the design through the George H. Mitchell Company of Chicago. Bock titled the piece *Defending the Flag*. Unfortunately, the monument exceeded the cost allowed by the state legislature. Determined that this design best suited their regiment, the veterans readily donated the remaining funds to make up the cost difference.

For thirty-six-year-old artist Richard W. Bock, this would be his first battlefield monument. The Chicago sculptor, born in Germany in July 1865, immigrated to the United States with his family at the age of five. During his teen years, Bock studied drawing at the Mechanics Institute of Chicago. In 1885, convinced that he had learned all he could about sculpture in Chicago, he headed to New York, where he quickly secured a job with Allen and Ketson. Bock worked with the company on the Vanderbilt House on Fifth Avenue. This would be his first taste of carving and sculpting for a home. Bock left New York to enroll in the Berlin Academy in Germany, where he spent a year studying art. In 1890, wishing to round out his studies, the sculptor went to Paris to study at the famed École des Beaux-Arts in Paris. After three years of study in Europe, Bock returned to the United States ready to work. In 1891, Chicago was preparing

Right: Wounded soldier
on the Seventy-ninth
Pennsylvania monument.
Photo by Jane D. Beal.

Below: Monument to
Knapp's Pennsylvania
battery on Orchard Knob
by Sylvester McCluskey.
Photo by Jane D. Beal.

for one of the biggest events in its history: the Columbian Exposition. Bock managed to secure a commission creating sculptures for the Mining and Metallurgy Building and the Electricity Building. With this job, he joined the ranks of other great upcoming artists who created short-lived masterpieces for the fair.

Shortly after completing the Seventy-ninth Pennsylvania monument, Bock made the acquaintance of a young Chicago architect named Frank Lloyd Wright. Wright would use Bock's designs for his innovative architecture. In 1896, the architect commissioned the artist to

Artist Richard W. Bock with a model for an Illinois monument at Shiloh National Military Park. *Courtesy of Richard W. Bock Museum, Greenville, Illinois, Sharon E. Grimes, director.*

create a plaster relief for the Isidore Heller House in Chicago. This was the beginning of a long working relationship between Wright and Bock. From 1891 to 1903, Bock would complete six public commissions, as well as numerous architectural sculptures, for Frank Lloyd Wright and many other noted architects.

Smith Granite accepted a contract for several designs and also had contracts with other states for monuments on the newly created battlefield park. Some of the designs came from stock molds; others submitted came from the creative minds of its talented artists. With so many monuments to create, only a few of its best sculptors could work on the Pennsylvania monuments. Edward L. Pausch, one of the company's most talented sculptors, created the Seventy-seventh Pennsylvania monument. The Copenhagen native began studying sculpture as a teenager at a granite company in Hartford, Connecticut. In 1889, skilled and experienced in working with clay and plaster, Pausch moved to Rhode Island and began working for Smith Granite.

While working for the Smith Company, he produced many of its works, including an equestrian statute of General George Washington for the city of Pittsburgh, Pennsylvania. It would be the first equestian state of Washington to be made entirely of granite. In 1900, the sculptor left the employ of Smith Granite to open his own studio.

As the monuments came to completion, the Pennsylvania commissioners began planning a dedication ceremony. Due to delays, they could not dedicate their monuments during the park dedication in September 1895. In 1897, they approached the Pennsylvania Assembly for money to transport the veterans to the battlefield for ceremonies. The bill passed without any arguments. The veterans would ride the railroad to Chattanooga free and could spend no fewer than five days visiting the monuments and sites. The Pennsylvania Assembly declared the dedication day as Pennsylvania Day.

Sculptor's studio at Smith Granite Company. It is believed that sculptor Edward Pausch is the man standing. Notice the models along the walls. *Courtesy of Babcock-Smith House in Westerly, Rhode Island.*

Dedication of the Pennsylvania monument. *Photo from* Pennsylvania at Chickamauga and Chattanooga: Ceremonies and Dedication of Monuments.

Survivors of the Seventy-ninth Pennsylvania posing in front of their monument, circa 1897. *Photo from* Pennsylvania at Chickamauga and Chattanooga: Ceremonies and Dedication of Monuments.

November finally arrived, and the aging veterans and their families boarded trains and traveled across the country to Chattanooga. The mayor of the city greeted the old soldiers and held a reception in their honor the first night after their arrival. Members of the local Grand Army of the Republic and the United Confederate Veterans greeted them with welcoming speeches. Both sides declared that the animosity of the past was long gone, and they now embraced one another as brothers. On November 13, the Pennsylvania delegation held exercises in the Chattanooga auditorium for a large crowd. Representatives of both veterans organizations gave more speeches. On the fifteenth, the veterans rode across the battlefield to their regimental monuments for dedication ceremonies. Knapp's battery dedicated its monument at Orchard Knob with addresses by former privates of the company. Of course, the monument's designer, Sylvester W. McCluskey, also attended. The Seventy-ninth and other regiments listened to speakers and then posed for photographs with their memorials. The men now would have their story told for all the future.

Indiana

The fallen heroes of the contesting armies sleep side by side. The surviving heroes of the mortal combat close hands in fraternal union across the once bloody chasm. Combatants then: comrades today—united now in a union to be disturbed no more.
—Indiana governor James Mount

The governor of Indiana, James Mount, a Chickamauga veteran, felt strongly that the State of Indiana should erect monuments memorializing the actions of the Indiana soldiers at the Battle of Chickamauga. Indiana ranked second in the number of military organizations engaged in the battle. More than ten thousand of the state's men fought, and more than three thousand fell. Indiana had more troops at Chickamauga than at any other battlefield at one time. It seemed natural and right that the state should remember its sons on the park with monuments telling their story.

In 1895, the state legislature passed a bill calling for the erection of monuments to mark the position of Indiana troops on the battlefields of Chickamauga, Missionary Ridge, Lookout Mountain and Chattanooga. The act also required the governor to appoint a committee of veterans of the battle to carry out the provision. After beginning work, the seven commissioners quickly realized that the legislature appropriated money only for monuments and markers on the Chickamauga battlefield. Therefore, the men could not erect monuments on the other fields. Dressed in their best business attire, the commissioners met with the national commission at the battlefield to locate fifty-five battle positions. They decided to meet again in May 1894 to continue locating battle lines.

The seven men returned to Indiana to begin the work of selecting monuments and gave the commissioners $32,000 to spend on appropriate memorials. The men soon realized that the funds would not allow them to place bronze monuments for all twenty-six regiments, and the cost of shipping made it prohibitive to use New England granite. After comparing costs, they applied for permission to use Indiana oolitic limestone. This would allow the commission

Eighth Indiana Infantry monument at Chickamauga. *Photo by Jane D. Beal.*

to erect larger, nicer monuments. To guarantee that each regiment
had a monument that best represented them on the battlefield, the
commissioners invited the veterans to meet with them to discuss the
erection of the memorials.

On May 21, 1895, the commissioners met with one or more
representatives of each regiment. The men suggested to the
veterans that each regiment create a committee to design their
monument and submit it to the commission. The men required
each design to include the state seal in bronze and to include a
historical tablet. Not wanting rivalry between veteran regiments,
the commissioners requested that the men not use supplemental
funds for the memorials. After reviewing each regiment's design,
the Indiana Commission awarded contracts to seven different
companies. American Bronze of Chicago received a contract for the
historical tablets. Noted architectural sculptor Albert L. Van Den
Berghen accepted the job for the state seals. This would be minor
work for the sculptor; at the time, the Chicago sculptor worked with
quickly rising architect Frank Lloyd Wright, creating sculptures for
architectural contracts. Setting the dedication to coincide with the
park dedication in September 1895, the commissioners required the
companies to complete their work by September 15 or receive a fine
of one dollar each day late.

Although it looked as though the State of Indiana was on its
way to erecting monuments in time for the park dedication, the
commission encountered difficulties that delayed the memorials for
three years. The park commissioners and the secretary of war had to
approve all inscriptions on the monuments. The Indiana inscriptions
consisted of battle details. This would create a controversy between
the state commissioners and the park commission, thus delaying the
completion of the memorials. The park commission disagreed with
the accuracy of the battle descriptions proposed. Commissioner
Frank Smith argued that the state committee disregarded the official
reports. Smith lamented to Park Historian Henry Boynton that it
appeared that the state committee merely took the most favorable
statements from the official reports for their monuments. He added
that it proved the old adage that "the pen is mightier than the
sword." Smith recommended that the state be allowed to only place

Eagle on top of an Indiana regimental monument. *Photo by Jane D. Beal.*

the state name, designation of the battery or regiment and the time of the position. He further recommended that the commissioner advise the secretary of war to enforce this regulation in the future as it pertained to the Chickamauga battlefield.

Disappointed that its monuments were not in place in time for the park dedication, the State of Indiana still participated in the park ceremonies. The park commission arranged for a campground near Cave Springs for the Indiana delegation, state officials and the veteran survivors. The state governor shipped tents for his staff and the veterans to use, and park engineers erected a speaker stand and seats. The park commission invited ex-president Benjamin Harris and former Indiana general Lew Wallace to give speeches. Not wanting to miss a chance to honor Indiana veterans and to correct his war record, Lew Wallace accepted. The former general was somewhat of a national celebrity. He had gained fame as the governor of New Mexico who had once offered the notorious Billy the Kid a pardon, and he had recently published the epic novel *Ben-Hur*. The general presented a speech extolling the virtues of reconciliation to an enthusiastic crowd of one thousand Indianans.

By fall of 1899, the State of Indiana finally had all its monuments in place with approved inscriptions. The Indiana Commission, which had replaced two members due to death, set the dedication date for September 20, 1899. The governor obtained an agreement with the railroad for a special rate of one cent per mile for the veterans and their families. Traveling by train and carriages, the veterans, wearing special ribbons commemorating the event, traveled to the Widow Glenn's field. The park commission erected a platform near the Wilder Monument in preparation for the ceremony. At 11:00 a.m., the president of the state commission, Captain D.B. McConnell, opened the event with a speech. As the birds chirped, the veterans of Indiana listened to speeches by the park historian, General Lew Wallace, General John. T. Wilder and members of the local Confederate Veterans Camp. Afterward, they traveled to the various regimental markers to reunite with old comrades and reminiscence of scenes long past.

Wilder Brigade Monument

General John T. Wilder's brigade formed a line at Widow Glenn's field in the afternoon of September 20, 1863. The Union men under Wilder poured thousands of rounds of ammunition into Confederate general Longstreet's men as they tried to push through the Union line. The numbers were too overwhelming; Wilder's men evacuated the field and retreated.

Long before most states began appointing commissions, and while the national commission was still forming the park, the veterans of Wilder's brigade began planning a monument for the Chickamauga battlefield. In late August 1890, four former officers met to plan an upcoming regimental reunion. In their discussions, General A.O. Miller suggested the idea of erecting a monument on the Chickamauga battlefield. It would be feasible if each regiment contributed $1,000 and each battery $500. The men loved the idea. Eager to begin, the officers wrote to General Wilder about their plan, and the general quickly agreed to help. He believed that his men, who had fought so valiantly on that day long ago, should have something to honor them. A year later, at the brigade reunion in Worthington, Indiana, the veterans organized a monument committee. General Wilder served as their treasurer.

Word spread quickly among the veterans. At the annual reunion of the Wilder Brigade Association, donations began to pour in. Drawing from their savings and earnings, the former union soldiers began sending donations to Wilder. Every dollar and quarter counted. By early 1892, the committee proudly announced that it had enough funds to arrange a contract for construction. Using a plan submitted by Harry Hargrove of Johnson City, Tennessee, the veterans chose to erect their monument on the hill in Widow Glenn's field. The monument, medieval in character, called for a 105-foot tower made from Chickamauga limestone. The top would feature a flagstaff. The soldiers decided to embed in it a steel safe to hold the brigade's archives. Wilder, who owned an iron foundry, added a wrought-iron gate to the entrance.

The Wilder's brigade monument. *Photo by Jane D. Beal.*

The veterans submitted their plan to the park commission for approval. The commissioners liked the monument and directed park engineer Betts to supervise the laying of the foundation. As the construction began in the spring of 1892, the donations continued to come in. General Wilder placed the money in a bank, and the construction moved quickly. The workers quarried stone for the monument from nearby Catfish Springs. As the tower grew, derricks and a motorized machine lifted the heavy limestone to the top. By 1893, the tower had reached a height of sixty feet.

Unfortunately, the 1890s were an economically volatile time in America. The economy crashed in 1893. The old veterans—some working, some having stopped by this point—began to limit their spending. Wilder received fewer and fewer donations. The general, an investor in an iron foundry and a tourist hotel in Johnson City, Tennessee, found his own cash flow slowed. To add to Wilder's concerns, the bank holding the money for the project failed. The veterans lost the entire $1,200 that they had raised for the monument. Construction came to a halt.

The veterans, growing older every year, patiently waited for the economy to improve. In 1895, realizing that many among their ranks were beginning to die, they began trying to raise more funds at the brigade reunion. Although they received some donations, it was not enough to begin construction again. The old soldiers became frustrated. They now had a half-completed monument and no funds to finish the work. By 1897, things looked bleak. Attending to business in Indianapolis, Wilder mentioned the situation to a young man named Arthur A. McKain. McKain, formerly in the monument business, had recently become successful by investing in a farming equipment company that made a straw stacker. Hearing of the plight of the Indiana veterans, the young businessman opened his checkbook and wrote the general a check for $1,200. He told the old general that he "was too young to take part in the war, so let me help in this matter by restoring to you the amount lost in the failure of the bank."

Elated and relieved, the veterans rehired the contractor and began work again. Park engineer Betts had misgivings about the height of the structure. In discussions with Boynton, both agreed

Left: The Wilder's brigade
under construction.
*Courtesy of Chickamauga
and Chattanooga National
Military Park.*

Below: Quarrying
limestone from Crawfish
Springs Quarry to
construct the Wilder's
brigade monument.
*Courtesy of Chickamauga
and Chattanooga National
Military Park.*

that the commission needed to reduce the size for structural safety. It was too late to do much remodeling, so Betts redesigned the monument and suggested that the height be limited to eighty feet. After discussions with the engineer, Wilder and the other veterans agreed to the design change. At the annual reunion in August 1898, the committee announced that the monument would be finished by 1899, and it made the young McKain an honorary member. Although the monument still lacked the stairs inside, the veterans dedicated the other Indiana monuments on September 20, 1899.

The veterans continued to solicit donations. By 1903, the monument stood complete with an iron staircase to the observation deck and the brigade's archives safely tucked away in the safe at the bottom. On September 20, 1903, the thinning ranks of Wilder's brigade survivors dedicated their completed monument. Wilder's grandson laid a wreath on the monument; their beloved commander did not live long enough to see the project completed.

New York

For we who wore the gray now wear the blue; we have taken the blue back into our colors and blue as far as the hand of man can make us, but look over the uncovered heads of the Grand Army of the Republic, the uncovered heads of the United Confederate Veterans, and you will see that the withering finger of time has touched us and we are all gray. A different gray from that we wore from 1862 to 1865—a gray rendered by a divine hand.
—*Colonel I. T. Dickenson*

The State of New York would spare no expense to honor its sons who had sacrificed so much. New Yorkers climbed the heights of Lookout Mountain and fought over Orchard Knob. The people of New York would not forget their sons' dedication and sacrifice on the faraway western battlefield. The state would use the peak of Lookout Mountain to create an everlasting symbol of peace and reconciliation.

New York state monument on Orchard Knob. *Photo by Jane D. Beal.*

New York was one of the first states to take immediate action on the call for monuments. In 1891, it formed the New York Monuments Commission, and former general Daniel Sickles took the honor of leading the commission. Sickles had served at Gettysburg, where many of his men fell, and he lost his leg. The commander's actions during the war earned him a Congressional Medal of Honor. After the war, he commanded a military district in the South during Reconstruction and served as an ambassador to Spain. Sickles's personal connection to the Gettysburg battle encouraged him to lead the efforts in preserving that battlefield. The commission first erected a monument at Gettysburg. However, Sickles was eager to honor and recognize the New York troops who served at Chattanooga as well.

The New York state legislature appropriated money for two monuments at Chattanooga. The commission went to work quickly to solicit designs. Unlike many other states, the veterans of the regiments did not select their own monuments. In September 1894, the New York Monuments Commission offered prizes to the winning designs. First place received fifty dollars, second place thirty dollars and third place twenty dollars. The New York commission selected a design for both monuments. The Bureau Brothers of Philadelphia contracted for the monuments, and the design for the memorials came from a sculptor by the last name of Burbere. The commission placed the largest monument near the Craven House on Lookout Mountain. The forty-five-foot-high monument would feature a bronze figure of a soldier doing picket duty. Commissioners selected Orchard Knob for the smaller monument. A soldier would surmount the Vermont granite monument, and a bronze state seal and tablets would adorn the lower portion. The monuments cost $10,000 each. By 1896, the memorials overlooked the bustling city of Chattanooga.

The top of Lookout Mountain, which gives a majestic view of the entire city, begged for a monument. The New York commission believed that it should be the one to place a monument on the mountain. Rumor in Chattanooga was that the state proposed to build a one-hundred-foot observation monument at Lookout Point. When the commission submitted an application for a monument at

New York monument near Craven House on Lookout Mountain. *Photo by Jane D. Beal.*

the summit of the mountain, the park commissioners debated the application. Regulations prohibited placing monuments or markers where the unit did not fight. During the fighting for the mountain, no troops made it to the summit. Commissioner Alexander Stewart rejected the proposal based on the clause in the regulations. The rest of the board approved the application because the state of New York did not propose a state monument or a regimental monument particularly; rather, it wished to erect a peace memorial. The park commission accepted the proposal due to the general nature of the monument and that it would recognize all troops regardless of which side they served.

The State of New York appropriated $80,000 for the proposed peace monument. Artist Roland Hinton Perry designed the ninety-five-foot monument. Perry, a native New Yorker, was becoming a noted artist. As a young boy, Perry began his formal study of art at the age of sixteen by enrolling in the Art Students League in New York City. After three years of study, he moved to Paris to study at the Academie Delecluse, focusing on sculpture. In 1890, Perry received admission into the renowned École des Beaux-Arts in Paris. He had the honor of being the only American admitted that year. After six years of study in France, the young sculptor returned to his home state of New York and accepted a commission to sculpt a bas-relief for the Library of Congress. One year later, he received the commission to create the *Court of Neptune* fount in

Above, left: Roland Hinton Perry. *Courtesy of American Archives of Art in Washington, D.C.*

Above, right: Bronze figures of a Northern soldier and a Southern soldier shaking hands. The statue, sculpted by Roland Hinton Perry, surmounts the top of the New York peace memorial on Lookout Mountain.

front of the library. His artistic ability earned him the contract for two monuments on the Gettysburg battlefield: the statues of Brigadier General George Greene and Brigadier General James Wadsworth. In all, Perry would create more than thirty major pieces of art, including the New York peace monument, before his death in 1941.

Perry's monument design called for a fifty-foot circular base, with a shaft surmounted by a bronze figure. Through a suggestion from General Sickles, the shaft included two figures of soldiers. One represented the North and the other the South. The eight-foot soldiers shook hands and offered each other peace. General Sickles described his design, with Old Glory towering by them: "Their hands once raised in strife, clasping a brother's hand." New York commissioner A.J. Zabriske, an engineer, drew up the specification plans for the massive memorial.

The work of designing the monument came easy compared to erecting such a large structure on top of the mountain. Somehow, the pink granite from Massachusetts and the Tennessee marble, along with the massive bronze figures and tablets, had to find their way to the top. To make the task easier, the park commissioners allowed the local contractor hauling the materials to lay a surface track up to the monument site. This would allow the workers to move the heavy stones directly to the top without having to stop and unload. The tracks were strictly for cars hauling stone and equipment, and the contractors needed to remove the tracks once finished.

Just the act of getting started created obstacles. Workers solved the issue of getting materials to the top, but the foundation created more problems. The New York commission wished to use broken limestone as the aggregate for the concrete foundation. The workers tried to use the hard surface stone of the summit of the mountain. The limestone proved impossible to break. After making three

Constructing the foundation for the peace memorial at Point Park on Lookout Mountain. *Courtesy of Chickamauga and Chattanooga National Military Park.*

The New York peace memorial. Erected by the New York Monuments Commission, the monument honors the soldiers of both sides. *Photo by Jane D. Beal.*

Laying the granite for the base of the peace memorial. *Courtesy of Chickamauga and Chattanooga National Military Park.*

attempts, the work crew gave up. Park engineer Betts decided that the best alternative would be to quarry the limestone from the nearby Cave Spring. The stones would then be broken into small pieces by hand.

In 1907, the completed $80,000 peace memorial rose majestically over Lookout Mountain. Unfortunately, the New York Monuments Commission would not dedicate the monument until 1910. The state appropriated $20,000 for the dedication ceremonies in Chattanooga. Negotiating a low rate, the state provided railroad service for the more than four hundred veterans and the New York delegation to travel to the battlefield. The group, headed by General Daniel Sickles, arrived on the evening of November 13, 1910. The following day, they visited the Wauhatchie battlefield and then traveled to Lookout Mountain after a light lunch. That evening, the veterans participated in a special program held at the Lyric Theater in downtown Chattanooga. The following day, many of the New Yorkers took the incline railroad to Point Park on the summit of the mountain. There they joined interested locals and the park commissioners in the dedication ceremonies of the peace memorial. After snapping photos and gazing out over the Tennessee Valley below, the group left, hoping that future generations would understand that the feelings of animosity were gone and that they prayed only for future peace.

ILLINOIS

Upon that field are the footprints of the sons of Illinois, and we have journeyed from afar place enduring monuments on the spots where they stood, where they fought, where they bled, and where hundreds of them died.
—*Illinois governor John P. Altgeld*

During the Civil War, Illinois raised regiments bearing the designations from Seventh to One Hundred Fifty-first. Only the One Hundred Twenty-first failed to organize. Many of these regiments experienced the horrors of war during the several days of fighting at Chickamauga. The Illinois soldiers, a mixture of seasoned veterans and some green recruits, took part in the battles from start to finish. During the early phase of the Chickamauga battle, a man from the Seventh Cavalry recalled that the bullets flew by so thick that they were as shelled corn scattered broadcast style. The fighting did not decrease in intensity the second day. The Twenty-second Illinois lost ninety-seven men within the first ten minutes of fighting. During the battle, the inexperienced Ninety-sixth Illinois lost a total of 8 officers and 220 men. Despite the horrific causalities, the Illinois troops would later participate in the November battles for Chattanooga.

During the early phase of the park's creation, the State of Illinois began assembling its commission. Governor John P. Altgeld appointed former major general John M. Palmer to head the commission. Palmer had commanded a division at Chickamauga and a corps at Chattanooga. He later became a governor and senator for the state. Altgeld also appointed other veterans of the battle, such as Major General John B. Turchin. In May 1895, the state appropriated $65,000 for markers and monuments on the battlefields. After careful consideration and study, the commission decided that each Illinois regimental monument would be identical in design. This would allow visitors to the battlefield to identify the Illinois positions with their eyes. By June 1896, Palmer and the rest of the commissioners submitted the design and inscriptions for fifty-three regimental monuments and fifty markers created by the J.S. Culver Construction Company of Springfield, Illinois, to the secretary of war. By 1897, the company had erected thirty-six memorials at Chickamauga, six monuments at Lookout Mountain and eleven more on Missionary Ridge—each constructed from dark Quincy granite.

The state only had one regimental monument that it did not erect. The survivors of the Nineteenth Illinois raised funds to erect their own memorial. The men who had fought so hard wanted to tell their story in their own manner. Keeping the design similar to the other Illinois monuments, the regiment decided to add a bas-relief depicting a battle scene. Captain David Bremmer, a successful banker, paid for the memorial to his regiment and hired Julia M. Brachen to sculpt the bas-relief. In 1887, Brachen, a native of Galena,

Illinois monument on Orchard Knob. *Photo by Jane D. Beal.*

Illinois monument on Missionary Ridge.
Photo by Jane D. Beal.

Illinois, began studying at the Chicago Institute of Art. While enrolled in the art institute, she became a student of Lorado Taft. In 1893, under Taft's tutelage, she created several of the white sculptures for the Columbian World Exposition in Chicago. She also received the commission to create the sculpture *Illinois Welcoming the World* for the Illinois building at the fair. People found the piece so beautiful that the governor had her duplicate it for the state capitol. In the regimental monument relief, Brachen depicted Bremmer and other members of the Nineteenth rushing Missionary Ridge and rallying around the American flag.

Not satisfied with just the markers and the regimental monuments, the veterans of Illinois proposed a state memorial on the battlefield of Chattanooga. In 1897, the state legislature appropriated funds to erect two monuments on the battlefield. The Illinois commissioners quickly began their search for appropriate designs and finally chose a design by Robert A. Ballard of Springfield, Illinois. Ballard worked in the capital city as an architect with his brother and had designed many prominent buildings in the city. The architect, working with the J.S. Culver Construction Company, won the contract for a large monument on Missionary Ridge. The monument would tower above the Bragg reservation near Bragg's headquarters site.

The eighty-foot white Barre granite monument featured four bronze figures at the base. Each figure represented a branch of the military. An allegorical sculpture of "Peace" graced the top of the monument. Ballard hired Norwegian artist Sigvald Asbjorn to sculpt the figures. Asbjorn exhibited great talent early in life. At the age of sixteen, he received a scholarship from the Norwegian king

A view of the Illinois monument on Missionary Ridge from the nearby
observation tower, circa 1900. *Courtesy of Chickamauga and Chattanooga National
Military Park.*

Oscar II to study art at the Royal Academy in Oslo. After studying
at the academy for five years, he immigrated to the United States to
practice art. Asbjorn opened his first studio in Michigan but moved
to Chicago a year later. Like many artists of period, the Norwegian
artist received a commission to work on the sculptures and buildings
for the Columbian World Exposition. Ballard requested Asbjorn to
create the sculpture of "Peace" for the top of the monument. The
figure grasped an olive wreath in one hand and an olive branch
in the other while gazing down on Missionary Ridge. Asbjorn
also sculpted the four base figures depicting an infantryman, a
cavalryman, an artillerist and an engineer.

The State of Illinois also erected a second state monument.
Although no Illinois troops fought on Orchard Knob, Illinois native
General Ulysses S. Grant used the site for his headquarters during
the Battle of Chattanooga. The state commission decided to place

a monument at Grant's headquarters to honor those who were not able to be in the line that swept the Confederates off Missionary Ridge. Again, the state contracted with J.S. Culver Construction Company for the monument. This design varied from the other Illinois monuments. The small, mausoleum-like structure featured a shaft with a bronze figure of a private on the top.

In 1899, with all the monuments complete, the State of Illinois appropriated $5,000 for dedication ceremonies at Chattanooga. On November 23, 1899, park commissioners, state dignitaries and the veterans gathered at Orchard Knob to dedicate the Illinois monuments. The Fifth Regimental band from Atlanta provided the music, and Park Historian Henry Boynton accepted the monuments on behalf of the government. A lone bugle sounded taps to close the ceremony. That evening, veterans gathered in Chattanooga for a symposium reviewing the late war and Illinois' role. The wives of the veterans attended a social event sponsored by the United Daughters of the Confederacy. The ill feelings of the past were gone, and the old soldiers and their families embraced one another as citizens of one country.

Iowa

The name Iowa appears conspicuously on nearly every face of each monument, so that when approached from any direction by friend or stranger, no one needs to ask "whose monument is this?"
—Iowa Commission

The rain drizzled down on the incline railway car. The elderly men and their wives and daughters prayed for the rain to stop. As they disembarked, they walked along the summit of Lookout Mountain, admiring the view and listening to the stories of the veterans. The day before, the group crowded into automobiles for an exciting tour along Missionary Ridge. Driving along Crest Road from the Bragg Reservation to Sherman Heights, they admired the view. Once again, the old soldiers told of the harrowing fight to claim the ridge years ago when they were spry young men defending their flag.

The governor of Iowa took great pride in honoring the Civil War veterans of his state. Upon the completion of monuments at Shiloh, Vicksburg, Andersonville and Chattanooga, he planned to honor the soldiers in a grand manner. Although not the first to respond to the call for monuments, Iowa put great effort in memorializing its sons' actions in the late war. During the Chickamauga-Chattanooga Campaign, Iowa lost seven commissioned officers and had two mortally wounded, as well as thousands of common soldiers killed. In 1894, the Twenty-fifth General Assembly of Iowa authorized the governor to appoint a five-man commission of veterans to mark Iowa's battle positions in the Chickamauga-Chattanooga Campaign. In September, the group traveled to Georgia and met with the park historian to review the Iowa locations and to select potential sites for monuments. The commissioners returned in September 1895 to attend the park dedication and compare notes with other state commissions.

The Iowa monument on Sherman Heights. *Photo by Jane D. Beal.*

After determining the Iowa positions and selecting potential sites for monuments, the commissioners submitted their report to the governor and the General Assembly. As part of their report, the men recommended that the legislature appropriate $20,000 to erect monuments on Lookout Mountain, as well as the right, left and center of Missionary Ridge. Perhaps due to the economic downturn, the General Assembly failed to appropriate any funds for monuments on the battlefield. Commissioner J.D. Fegan wrote to the governor urging him to push for money in the next session.

Iowa monument near the Craven House on Lookout Mountain. *Photo by Jane D. Beal.*

Fegan, anxious to begin work, expressed concern that they should begin erecting monuments very soon while the battle participants could "supervise the work."

Despite the commissioner's recommendations and decrease in battle survivors, the state legislature failed to respond. In 1902, the General Assembly finally passed legislation to appoint another commission to erect three monuments at Chattanooga and Chickamauga. It also appropriated $35,000 for the task. Governor Albert Cummins immediately appointed eleven men to serve as commissioners. Among those appointed was Alonzo Abernathy, who served with the Ninth Iowa. Abernathy would act as the commission's secretary. After reviewing previous recommendations, the new commissioners quickly decided on three locations. One monument would be located at Sherman Heights, another would be near the Craven House on Lookout Mountain and the third would be near Rossville Gap.

The commission awarded a contract to Van Amringe of Boston, Massachusetts, for the monuments. The design for the Sherman Heights and the Lookout Mountain monuments called for a large shaft, with a figure of a soldier holding or guarding the flag at the top. Both monuments rose into the sky to the height of fifty feet. The Lookout Mountain memorial featured a fifteen-foot-square base and sat just below the Craven House. The monument denoted the farthest position Iowa troops reached during the battle. The commission selected a spot near the summit of Sherman Heights for the other memorial. Iowa troops had captured this spot during the battle of Missionary Ridge on November 25, 1863. This monument featured a fifteen-foot octagonal base and a soldier guarding the flag at the top of the shaft.

Although the Iowa soldiers did not engage in intensive combat in Rossville Gap, they did have a special connection to the site. After the battle of Lookout Mountain, the Iowa troops marched down from the mountain and in review in Rossville Gap. The commissioners selected the site of where General Peter Osterhaus reviewed the Iowa troops. However, the location chosen for the memorial did not belong to the government. The park owned land on the northeast end of Missionary Ridge and about fifty feet of the roadway on the south end. The Iowa Commission would have to purchase the land for its monument. The commissioners quickly learned that the local landowners were not willing to donate their land and charged unreasonable prices. This proved true with the first tract of land that the commission tried to purchase. The Iowa men chose another site. Because the government would not accept the monument unless it was on federal property, the State of Iowa deeded the land to the United States government.

Obtaining the land proved a minor issue compared to the actual construction of the Rossville Iowa monument. This would be the largest of the Iowa monuments. The completed monument would stand seventy-two feet high on a twenty-foot-wide octagonal base. Four corners of the monument would feature granite statues of soldiers. The top of the shaft would have a statue as well. The Van Amringe Company, which fulfilled the contract, shipped the large pieces of Barre granite by train to the site, and the work crew lifted the heavy stone into the air using derricks. Unfortunately, through mishandling, the shaft fell and broke. As it fell, the stone broke several pieces of the granite base. Van Amringe estimated the damage to be between $3,000 and $4,000. The contractor shipped the granite shaft back to Vermont and ordered a duplicate piece. The second one arrived in Rossville, only to have Amringe's men reject it. After inspection, the contractor found that the stone had too much iron and was unusable. The workers boxed the piece back up and left it at the side of the road. The granite company ordered a third piece of stone the same as the first two pieces. A few weeks later, the third piece of granite arrived, and with much anticipation, the workers hoisted it into place. Finally, the last of the Iowa monuments was complete, and the state could hold dedication ceremonies.

By 1906, the State of Iowa had erected monuments at Shiloh, Vicksburg, Chattanooga and Andersonville. Governor Albert Cummins decided that the best way to honor the Civil War veterans and dedicate all of the monuments would be through a tour of the South. A joint committee appointed by the governor arranged for a special train to take the governor's staff, the state commissioners, the veterans and their families to all four sites for ceremonies. The Fifty-fifth Iowa band joined the group to provide music. For two weeks, 150 Iowans traveled across the South, remembering their soldiers.

The tour began with dedication ceremonies at the Shiloh battlefield. To reach the park, the entourage took the train to Johnsonville, Tennessee, and then took a steamer to Pittsburg Landing, Tennessee. After the dedication ceremony at Shiloh, the group boarded the train and traveled to Vicksburg, Mississippi, for dedications. During the trip across the South to Andersonville and the other sites, the men gathered every evening in the smoking car to refight the late war's battles. One member of the group recalled that the veterans "scrapped earnestly, each man contending that he was right and claiming the other didn't know a thing about it."

After a brief dedication at the site of the former prisoner of war camp, the entourage headed to Chattanooga. Upon arrival, the Iowans immediately took automobiles to Sherman Heights, Lookout Mountain and Missionary Ridge. For many, it would be one of their first adventures in an automobile. The rough, muddy roads leading to Missionary Ridge created problems for the group. A few of the cars experienced flat tires. After several flats, many members of the group who had no experience changing a tire decided to walk back to town to catch a streetcar. At least one group managed to repair its flat and continue on the tour. A member of the group commented that during their visit to Chattanooga, they had received a practical education in "the noble art of replacing automobile tires, which in this day and age should form a considerable part of every man's practical education."

After a band concert in Chattanooga by the Fifty-fifth Iowa band, the Iowans gathered the following morning on Lookout Mountain to dedicate the monument. A light drizzle and fog made the paths to the monument challenging and the remarks brief. The old veterans, knees creaking and muscles aching, climbed down to catch the incline railway to the bottom. After

Fifty-fifth Iowa regimental band at the Iowa monument near Rossville. *Photo from Dedicating in Dixie.*

lunch, the skies cleared, and the group gathered at Sherman Heights along Missionary Ridge for another dedication ceremony. On the afternoon of November 20, 1906, the Iowa veterans and state dignitaries gathered at the Rossville monument for the main dedication of the Iowa monuments. The band played rousing patriotic music, and Governor Cummins accepted the monument from the Iowa Commission. The governor presented the beautiful Iowa monuments to the United States government. After the ceremony, the group gathered around the Rossville monument, admiring the stone soldiers guarding the mountains. They posed for photos, and the old soldiers reminisced one last time about their hard-won victory in the "battle above the clouds." The following day, the delegation from Iowa boarded the train and returned to its home state.

Wisconsin

*We should come to this work with more than a sense of duty or
privilege. We should come to it as a work of love. Love for our
old commonwealth and the heroic deed of her sons, living or dead!*
—*Archibald Blakely of Pennsylvania*

The women laughed and talked as they admired the granite
horse. A slight breeze tugged at their enormous hats, but the
hatpins kept them firmly in place. The gentleman traveling with
them told the women to stand still. He adjusted his camera and
took a photo. Now they would have a souvenir of their visit to the
Chickamauga battlefield. They climbed back into their automobile
and finished touring the park. The threesome stopped at each
Wisconsin monument to remember the old soldiers from their
home state.

The First Wisconsin Cavalry monument is one of the most
photographed monuments at Chickamauga. Each time a
person snaps a photo and reads the inscription, the bravery of
Wisconsin's soldiers is retold. The soldiers would be overjoyed
to know that more than one hundred years later, visitors
continue to admire their monuments. In 1893, the Wisconsin
legislature formed a commission to mark the Wisconsin lines
on the Chickamauga battlefield. The five-man commission met
regularly and reviewed the post-battle reports. In March 1893,
the men traveled to Georgia to visit with the national commission
to locate Wisconsin's battle lines. As the commissioners wandered
over the battlefield, recalling the bloody battle, they met members
of the Ohio Commission. The Ohio delegation was visiting the
battlefield to locate its troop positions as well. Satisfied with the
locations, the Ohio commission planned to return home and ask
for funds to erect monuments. The Wisconsin commissioners
agreed that the state troops needed some type of memorial. The
men requested money and received an appropriation of $20,000.
Elated with the sum, the commissioners visited the Chickamauga
battlefield again. This time, the men examined the monuments
erected by Ohio for ideas.

Wisconsin state monument.

By 1895, excited with the prospect of honoring the state's troops with memorials, the Wisconsin appointees sent out a request for bids and designs. That April, the commissioners met again to examine the numerous proposals. Wishing to honor

First Wisconsin Cavalry monument. The memorial depicts a riderless horse. *Photo by Jane D. Beal.*

each individual unit, the men selected unique designs and awarded contracts to several companies. The Smith Granite Company received a contract for three infantry and two batteries monuments. The J.A. Anderson Company accepted a contract for two monuments, and the commission selected two designs submitted by the Marrison Granite Company.

The Wisconsin Commission allotted approximately $1,700 for each infantry monument and $1,200 for battery monuments. Perhaps it was due to the beauty of the design that caused the commissioners to allocate $1,900 for the First Wisconsin Cavalry monument. Marrison Granite submitted a design for a riderless horse featuring bronze reins, bit and bridle. The members of the commission and First Wisconsin Cavalry immediately contemplated placing an iron fence around the horse, fearing damage from well-intentioned visitors. Edward Pausch, who worked as a sculptor for Smith Granite, inspired the commissioners with his granite soldier on the Tenth Wisconsin monument. The artist left out few details on the flag or the soldier's face. By November 1895, all the monuments graced the battlefield, and the commissioners returned to inspect them.

Satisfied with their work, the men felt that the Wisconsin soldiers needed some recognition for their part in the battles for Chattanooga. In May 1897, after requesting funds, the state legislature passed a bill authorizing the erection of a monument on the Chattanooga battlefield. The commissioners selected a spot on Orchard Knob just south of Grant's headquarters. The following June, the men met again to review the designs submitted for the proposed monument. Unhappy with the proposals, they rejected all of them and sent out another request. The following month, the commissioners reviewed the new designs and selected a simple, but elegant, design by Buemming and Dick of Milwaukee.

The Wisconsin Commission wished to dedicate the monuments as soon as possible. The number of survivors shrank with each passing year. The commissioners selected July 24, 1889, for the dedication ceremonies. Due to the war with Spain, Wisconsin troops were drilling and training on the Chickamauga battlefield. Wishing to give some added entertainment, the commissioners requested permission to use the Wisconsin troops at Camp Thomas near Chattanooga. The Wisconsin commander agreed and believed that the march to Orchard Knob for the ceremony would be good practice. On the set day, the Wisconsin troops marched to the ceremonies, impressing the crowd with their military precision. Former Wisconsin soldier Samuel Fallows opened the speeches with a prayer. The old veterans and their families gathered around their state monument as they listened to the speeches and formally presented their memorial to the federal government.

United States Regular Troops

*The bitterness and resentments of the war belong to the past. Its
glories are the common heritage of us all.*
—Governor William McKinley

These men represented no particular state. They enlisted in the
United States Army to serve not just their state but also their
country. State volunteers did most of the fighting at the Battles
of Chattanooga and Chickamauga. Largely overlooked are the
seven Regular federal troops. The Fourth United States Cavalry,
the Fourth and Fifth U.S. Artillery and the Fifteenth, Sixteenth,
Eighteenth and Nineteenth U.S. Infantry served at the Battles of
Chickamauga and Chattanooga. Largely organized in 1861, these
troops served during the entire war. Long after the commanders
signed peace agreements, many of these regular troops continued
to serve the country.

Park guidelines called for states to mark troop positions and erect
monuments to their troops. Because the Regular Army served no
particular state, the park commission worked to memorialize the
actions of the U.S. regular troops. The establishing regulations
required the national commission to mark the troop positions
and erect monuments to the federal troops. The United States
government provided funding for the monuments as part of the
appropriation for the park.

The park commissioners called on the former members of
the troops to help with positioning and selecting memorials. In
June 1892, eight officers representing the regiments and batteries
traveled the battlefield to choose locations for their memorials.
After selecting the sites, the officers returned home to draw up
sketches for designs and to write the inscriptions. Upon approval,
the park commissioners contracted with Smith Granite to create
the monuments. The granite company, actively bidding for several
state contracts, began work immediately. The company contracted
with Bureau Brothers Foundry of Pennsylvania for the bronze work.
The foundry, owned by two French immigrant brothers, Achille
and Edouard, had developed a reputation for superior bronze

work. Since arriving in the country in the 1870s, the two men had completed numerous bronze sculptures for prominent artists.

The Smith Company assigned some of its best artists to work on the seven monuments. One of those was its best cutter, Columbus Zerbarini. In 1865, Zerbarini arrived in the United States with his brother, Angelo, his father and his uncle. The two young brothers studied stonecutting in New York, and their talent led them to jobs with the New England Granite Works. In 1881, the two men moved to Westerly, Rhode Island, and began working for Smith Granite. Zerbarini worked skillfully on the Sixteenth United States Infantry monument, creating a detailed sculpture of a soldier in the act of aiming his rifle.

In June 1893, the park commission happily reported that the seven memorials to the regular troops were complete and erected on the battlefield. In late 1893, the commission erected two more monuments to the regular troops on the battlefield. Amazingly, the beautiful works cost the park only about $2,000 each. In September 1895, the nine monuments received their dedication as part of the grand ceremonies for the park.

Part IV

CONFEDERATE AND BORDER STATE MONUMENTS

*But their memories e'er shall remain for us, And their names, bright
names, without stain for us: The glory they won shall not wane for us,
In legend and lay;
Our heroes in Gray
Shall forever live over again for us.*
—Abram Joseph Ryan

The former Confederate States of America dissolved at the end
of the Civil War. Without the Confederacy, the task of erecting
memorials to the Southern soldiers fell to the states and private
organizations. The economic swings of the late nineteenth century
left the southern economy struggling to regain strength. With little
extra funds available, only a few states erected monuments on key
battlefields. Henry Boynton and Ferdinand Van Derveer partially
chose to preserve the Chickamauga and Chattanooga battlefields
because both sides could claim a victory. Being the first battlefield
park, the site allowed both sides to show that they no longer harbored
anger and bitterness toward each other, but rather only wanted
reconciliation and a united nation. Even with limited funds, many
southern state governments appropriated large sums of money to
tell of the soldiers' victory and sacrifice on the battlefields.

Kentucky

*As we are united in life and they united in death, let one monument
perpetuate their deeds, and one people forgetful of all asperities,
forever hold in grateful remembrance all of the glories of the
terrible conflict which made all men free of the glories of the
terrific war, which made all men free and retained every star on
the nation's flag.*

—*inscription on the Kentucky monument*

The state of Kentucky struggled with divided loyalties during the
war. Many of its citizens were slaveholders, while many others
opposed the practice of slavery. Refusing to leave the Union to
join the Confederacy, the state nonetheless faced its own internal
conflict during the war. Young men eagerly rushed to arms and
joined regiments of both armies. The first lady, Mary Todd Lincoln,
a Kentucky native, found her own loyalties often in question because
she came from a Southern family. Her dearly beloved brother-in-
law, Benjamin Hardin Helms, died at the Battle of Chickamauga
while serving in a Confederate Kentucky regiment. After the war,
Kentucky joined many other borders states in trying to rebuild and
develop reconciliation among its residents.

During the Battle of Chickamauga, Kentucky regiments fought
on both sides. When the park commission sent out notice to the
states to form commissions to mark the battlefield, Kentucky quickly
responded, wanting to honor soldiers of both sides. In 1893, wanting
to ensure that the actions of Kentucky were not forgotten, the state
legislature passed a resolution to create a commission. The group
worked with the park commissioners in locating battle positions and
attended the park dedication in 1895. Unlike many other states,
Kentucky did not appropriate money for monuments at that time.
Perhaps the state budget prevented allocating the extra money.

In early 1898, the State of Kentucky finally decided to honor
its soldiers with a monument at Chickamauga. The legislature
appropriated about $13,000 for a memorial. In June 1898, working
with the Muldoon Monument Company of Louisville, Kentucky,
the commission created a memorial unlike any others erected on the

Top, left: Kentucky state monument at Chickamauga. *Photo by Jane D. Beal.*

Top, right: Rear view of the bronze statute Bellona, the goddess of war, on top of the Kentucky monument.

Bottom: Rampaging tiger head representing battle on the Kentucky state monument.

park at that time. The state wanted to honor all its men, regardless
of the side for which they fought. The Kentucky commissioners
explained that they wanted their monument to be of a distinctive
military character and not to offend the sensibilities of friends of
either cause. Therefore, they chose to use allegorical figures. On the
front of the cap over the die, the monument design called for crossed
Union and Confederate flags. An eagle grasped a staff and spread
its wings over both flags. The committee placed a Confederate
shield with laurel wreaths on one side and on the opposite side
placed a Union shield. The head of a rampaging tiger jutted out
from the four corners. The tiger symbolized battle. A bronze statue
of Bellona, the goddess of war, stood on a sphere at the top. The
sphere rested on four cannons pointing out at different angles. The
commission selected the goddess so that it could "obviate the use
of the stereotyped soldier, which might cause dissension." Worried

Above, left: Kentucky monument under construction. *Courtesy of Chickamauga and
Chattanooga National Military Park.*

Above, right: The Kentucky monument veiled before the dedication ceremony.
Courtesy of Chickamauga and Chattanooga National Military Park.

The unveiling of the Kentucky monument during the dedication ceremony on
May 3, 1899. *Courtesy of Chickamauga and Chattanooga National Military Park.*

about the longevity and safety of the monument, the commissioners
chose to place all the embellishments high enough to be out of the
reach of possible vandals.

Delighted with Kentucky's design, the park commission quickly
approved of the Barre granite monument. The proposed inscriptions

took longer for approval. Kentucky wished to place on the front, "Erected by the state of Kentucky. In memory of her sons who fought and fell on this field. Love and tears for the blue. Tears and love for the gray." The last two lines created some objections among the park commissioners. One argued that the regulations called for all inscriptions to be historical in nature and that, in the past, the commission denied partisan inscriptions. Henry Boynton argued to the secretary of war that park regulations did not necessarily require inscriptions to be historical in nature and that the lines were bipartisan. Boynton further added that the Kentucky monument was the first monument to honor troops from both sides. The secretary of war left the approval to Boynton and the park commission.

On May 3, 1899, Kentuckians and residents of the Chickamauga and Chattanooga area gathered on the battlefield for the unveiling and dedication of the Kentucky monument. A large cloth covered the monument so that crowds would have to wait to see the magnificent memorial. After speeches lauded the efforts and valor of both sides of the war, the governor's daughter unveiled the monument. The crowd applauded and greatly admired the forty-four-foot monument to Kentucky's sons.

Maryland

Yonder monument stands as a symbol of peace and unity, a tribute to heroic valor, dedicated to the memory of men who have measured up to the highest standard of American manhood.
—Captain John R. King

Sitting between free and slave states, Maryland split during the war. While many citizens owned slaves, plenty of others opposed the institution and even the thought of secession. On the Chattanooga battlefield, Maryland troops served both sides. After the war, the people of the state worked to overcome the ill feelings and bitterness. The erection of monuments on the battlefields provided a physical symbol of their reconciliation.

The Maryland monument on Orchard Knob.

Maryland was not one of the first states to appoint a commission to mark the battlefield park. The state legislature did not take up the cause of erecting monuments until 1900, when it appointed a commission to erect a monument on the Antietam battlefield. Two years later, the Maryland legislature appropriated $7,000 for monuments and markers on the Chickamauga-Chattanooga National Military Park. The enabling legislation authorized the governor to appoint a commission to mark the battle lines and honor the Third Maryland Volunteer Infantry and Latrobe's Confederate battery.

The governor appointed a group of veterans from Maryland to serve as state commissioners. The president of the commission, Benjamin F. Taylor, knew the process of erecting a monument well. Taylor, who served with the Second Maryland during the war, assisted in erecting the state's monument at Antietam. Seven men accepted appointments and began immediately working to erect a suitable monument, and they all agreed that the memorial should honor soldiers of both sides. After visiting the battlefield, the commissioners selected a site on Orchard Knob.

Upon reviewing the hundreds of design proposals, the commissioners selected one large monument. The Van Amringe Granite Company not only submitted a fitting design that met the budget, but it also had considerable experience erecting monuments on the battlefield. Van Amringe built one each of the Ohio and the Iowa monuments. The commissioners originally suggested using Guilford granite from Maryland. The Van Amringe Company recommended the often-used Westerly granite, and Maryland agreed. The company's design called for a fifteen-foot base, with a shaft rising to the height of forty-four feet. Halfway up the shaft, a laurel wreath, symbolizing peace, encircled the monument. A color bearer at parade rest and holding a Federal flag surmounted the entire monument. To symbolize and honor soldiers of both armies, the design included six-foot statues on either side of the base. On the right stood a Confederate artilleryman holding a sponge and shading his eyes while he peered into the smoke of battle. A Federal infantryman stood on the opposite side. The infantryman held his gun at rest

View of the Maryland monument with the Illinois monument in the background, circa 1910. *Courtesy of the Hamilton Country Library.*

but had his other hand over his cartridge box as if he were ready to respond to the command "handle cartridge."

By July 1903, the contractor had finished the impressive monument. The Maryland commissioners began making plans for a dedication ceremony on October 8, 1903. Chartering a special train, the commissioners, veterans and representatives of the Maryland governor traveled to Tennessee for the ceremony. Arriving in Chattanooga at nine o'clock in the morning, the delegation had little time for taking in the sights before the program. The ceremony began promptly at noon. After the park commissioner accepted the monument on behalf of the government with an elegant speech, the Maryland entourage embarked on a tour of the battlefield. Resting in a hotel in downtown Chattanooga, the party left early the next morning to return home. Although it was only one monument, future park visitors would remember the valor of the Maryland soldiers for generations.

Tennessee

Let your sons study the lives and characters of these and many others of our great and heroic men; and your daughters, those of the many noble confederate women who illustrated the loftiest traits of the truest Christian womanhood, who deserve to be and were, the wives, the mothers and sisters of a race of heroes.
—Alexander P. Stewart

The men gathered on the top of Snodgrass Hill were showing signs of age. It took great effort for many of them to walk across the battlefield to the dedication site. These men did not mind the exertion, though. After many years, they were finally dedicating monuments in honor of themselves and their comrades who died so long ago. The bitterness of the past had left them. Now the Tennesseans only wanted to ensure that future Americans did not forget their actions.

Tennessee Artillery monument. *Photo by Jane D. Beal.*

Tennessee, the last state to join the Confederacy, became the first southern state to dedicate monuments on the Chickamauga battlefield. Like Kentucky and Maryland, Tennesseans were divided over leaving the Union. Governor Isham G. Harris and the

Tennessee legislatures voted to secede and join the Confederacy. Tennessee residents held divided loyalties. Many east Tennesseans supported the Union and raised regiments for the Federal army. West and middle Tennessee raised both Confederate and Union regiments. About 25 percent of the Tennessee soldiers serving in the Civil War fought for the Union army. Honoring its sons would be a delicate task for the state.

On March 11, 1893, a joint House resolution passed authorizing the governor to appoint a committee to locate the positions of Tennessee troops on the Chickamauga and Chattanooga battlefields. To be fair and have equal representation, the bill required that the three sections of the state have a representative. In April 1894, the committee met in Nashville to organize itself. The following May, the commissioners examined the battlefield and located positions. After finding battle sites, the men submitted a report to the state legislature recommending money be appropriated for monuments to the Tennessee troops.

Despite the struggling economy, the Tennessee legislature passed an act appropriating $10,000 for monuments and markers to the Tennessee troops. The governor appointed a new commission consisting of nine former soldiers. Captain Willam Bate, a former governor and senator from Tennessee, temporarily chaired the committee. In July 1895, Bate called a meeting of the commissioners. All agreed that the state should erect monuments honoring troops from both sides of the conflict, and before adjourning, the men drew up an advertisement for bids.

Eager to see the designs, the Tennesseans gathered again in September 1895. Many of the large granite companies presented designs, including Smith Granite Company, Morris Brothers of Memphis and Muldoon Monument Company. One company from Knoxville also presented bids. The Knoxville Company advised the commissioners to use Tennessee granite, arguing that it was just as durable as granite from Vermont or elsewhere. After a lengthy review process, the commission settled on four designs, and the men agreed that the memorials should be of Tennessee gray granite. Major C.W. Anderson moved that the figures be of bronze. The design called for four identical bases and pedestals. Each would feature a fourteen-foot, four-inch bronze statue. Three of the monuments would honor the Tennessee Confederate artillery, cavalry and infantry. Because only a Tennessee Union cavalry regiment served in the battle, the commission would honor its men with a monument featuring a cavalry soldier.

Entering into a contract with the Muldoon Monument Company, the Tennesseans eagerly awaited the completion of the memorials. Shortly after beginning, the commission encountered a difficulty. It had selected land along Scott's yard for the Confederate cavalry monument. However, the property did not belong to the United States government, and all monuments had to be on federal property. After several attempts, the national commission remained unable to acquire the land. The Tennesseans changed the location of the monument to some property near Cloud Spring. The owner of the property, wishing to assist the old veterans, donated the land to the federal government. In May 1896, the Muldoon Monument Company reported to the commission that the memorials were complete. Despite having the monuments in place, the state did not immediately hold a dedication ceremony. Finally, on May 12, 1898, the veterans of Tennessee dedicated the monuments. In his address, former general Alexander P. Stewart remarked how their ranks were thinning and soon the Confederate veteran would only be a memory.

Georgia

Around it sleep slayer and slain
All the brave, all sinking to rest
Convinced of duty done.
Glorious battlefield! Blessed Peace!
—Major Joseph B. Cummings

The veterans of Georgia gathered around the flag-draped monument, eager to see it revealed. Thirty-six years earlier, the

Georgians fought a hard and bloody battle on the very ground where they were now standing. Despite the victory, many had died and others were wounded. The ribbons denoting the Georgian veterans flapped in the breeze, and their summer straw hats shaded their eyes. As the minister said the prayer, the audience bowed their heads in reverence of the living and dead soldiers. Georgia Major Joseph B. Cummings's inscription on the monument best summed up the purpose of the gathering as being in remembrance of "those who fought and lived and those who fought and died those who gave much and those who gave all."

The Battle of Chickamauga was a victory for the South and for Georgia. The State of Georgia provided the Confederacy with twenty-eight units during the battle, many of which took heavy causalities. Some southern states hesitated to appropriate money for marking the battlefield and especially for a monument. The State of Georgia, though, responded with enthusiasm. On December 15, 1894, the state legislature approved a bill calling for a commission of Georgia veterans to inspect the battlefield and locate the position of its troops. It also gave them the authority to mark the lines with appropriate monuments. Later, in May 1896, the Georgia legislature resolved to erect one grand and imposing monument somewhere near the center of the battlefield and to erect fifty-five battle monuments. The resolution also called for the creation of a five-person state memorial board. General Gordon Lee and W.S. Everett, the latter of whom commanded an artillery battery during the battle, accepted two-year terms on the board. Major Joseph B. Cumming, who served with the Army of Tennessee from its inception until it surrendered, and Colonel James S. Boynton, a veteran of the battle and former Georgia governor, accepted four-year positions.

After meeting with park commissioners at the Crawfish Springs Hotel, the board decided to advertise for design and specification bids. With $20,000 to spend for the memorial, the committee began the process of selecting a monument. Offering the winning bidder $500, twenty-four companies from across the nation submitted proposals. At a meeting on September 10, 1896, at the park hotel, the board listened to each company explain the merits of its design.

Georgia state monument. *Photo by Jane D. Beal.*

Derricks lift the bronze figure into place on top of the Georgia monument.
Courtesy of Chickamauga and Chattanooga National Military Park.

Detail of the horses heads along the capstone of the Georgia monument. *Photo by George A. Reaves IV.*

At the end of the day, the men settled on ten proposals, and after much discussion and review, they selected a design by the Muldoon Monument Company of Louisville, Kentucky. To get the best-quality work, the men also advertised for the bronze work separate from the granite. The board hired Gorham Foundry in New York for the bronzes.

The selected design featured a bronze sculpture of a Confederate soldier holding a furled Confederate flag and pointing to the distance. Four bronze figures representing the branches of service graced the base. Hiring sculptor Frederick Moynihan of New York, the bronze work took more than a year to complete. Moynihan, born on the island of Guerney in 1843, came from a family and village of granite stonecutters and sculptors. As a young man, he left his home to study art at the Royal Academy of Art in London. In 1881, Moynihan immigrated to the United States and opened his own studio. He quickly found work creating portrait sculptures

Above, left: The bronze statue surmounting the Georgia monument.

Above, right: Georgia monument draped with an American flag prior to the
dedication ceremony on May 10, 1899. *Courtesy of Chickamauga and Chattanooga
National Military Park.*

for Civil War monuments and took commissions for memorials at
Gettysburg and the Ninth Pennsylvania "Lochiel" veteran cavalry
monument at Chickamauga prior to the Georgia monument. In
1904, he began his most famous work: the equestrian statue of
J.E.B. Stuart in Richmond.

The Georgia Memorial Board decided early that the granite for
the monument had to be from the state. The men finally settled
on Georgia blue granite. The Muldoon Monument Company
subcontracted with the Venerable Brothers Granite Company.
Brothers Samuel and William owned the quarry at Stone
Mountain, Georgia. For the monument, the company quarried
stone from the foot of Stone Mountain and shipped it to Muldoon
Company. In 1898, after careful construction and oversight, the
sixty-three-foot, five-inch memorial stood complete and ready for
dedication. The day prior to the ceremony, the Georgia governor

Dedication of the Georgia state monument on May 10, 1899. *Courtesy of Hamilton County Library.*

and veterans attended the Kentucky monument dedication. On May 10, 1899, Georgians, Tennesseans and Kentuckians gathered around the Georgia monument. The board draped the memorial with an American flag. The state may have fought for the Confederacy, but now they were all American. A band roused the crowd with patriotic songs. The governor and members of the board presented speeches honoring the actions of the Georgia soldiers. Finally, the flag lifted and revealed the stunning bronzes, and the park commission accepted the monument on behalf of the federal government. Georgia had ensured that its sons would never be forgotten at Chickamauga.

South Carolina

*Official reports and history record the glory of the leaders who
fell, but only the weeping mother, the sorrowing wife or the
faithful comrade preserve the name—engraved on their heart—of
the humble private, who gave his life for the country he loved.*
          —General William H.T. Walker

South Carolina was the first state to secede from the Union,
and its troops fought hard for their cause. During the Battle of
Chickamauga, South Carolina troops fought in some of the fiercest
of the fighting. The men of the Palmetto State assaulted the Union
lines on Snodgrass Hill with determination. After rushing across
an eight-hundred-yard field to attack the Federal lines, the South
Carolina soldiers swept the enemy from the hill and eventually
helped the Rebels win the battle.

Perhaps because it was a Southern victory, or because of its
terrible losses, South Carolina responded to the call to mark the
new battlefield park. In May 1894, the state legislature appointed a
committee to locate the troop positions on the battlefield. Veterans
of Kershaw's brigade; the Tenth, Nineteenth, Twenty-fourth South
Carolina; and Culpepper's battery served on the committee. They
visited the battlefield and met with the park commission, as well as
General Thomas Wilder, Colonel J.S. Gill and Captain Heron of
Ohio. The men traveled the battlefield and compared their notes
and memories. The commission reported to the legislature that it
believed that the park commission had done an excellent job in
marking the battlefield, and it recommended that the state erect a
monument to the South Carolina troops.

Acting on the recommendation of its commission, the South
Carolina legislature appointed a second commission. The men
selected for this committee would select a design for a monument
and markers. The appointed men met and advertised for proposals.
After a review of bids, they selected a design. However, the state
did not appropriate money to erect the monument. Perhaps due
to money constraints, South Carolina waited to appropriate money
for a memorial at Chickamauga. During the 1899 convention of

South Carolina state monument. *Photo by Jane D. Beal.*

the South Carolina division of the United Confederate Veterans, a member made a motion to memorialize the soldiers on the Chickamauga battlefield. The aging veterans began to lobby their state representatives to erect a monument in their honor. The strategy worked. On February 17, 1900, the state passed a bill authorizing the governor to appoint a committee of three Confederate veterans and the adjutant general to erect a monument on the battlefield "to perpetuate the heroic deeds and devotion of our state." This time, it also authorized $10,000 for the memorial.

The memorial committee visited the battlefield to select the best spot for a monument. The men all left in agreement to place the memorial on the rise northwest of Dyer Field on the foothills of Snodgrass Hill. One commissioner remarked that the "knoll is one of, if not the most, striking points on the field." While visiting Georgia, the men put out a call for designs and bids, and upon reviewing the proposals, the committee awarded a contract to Stewart Stone Company of Columbia, South Carolina. The company impressed the men with its design and low bid. The veterans selected a monument similar to a memorial on the South Carolina Statehouse grounds raised in memory of the Palmetto Regiment. The Stewart design called for a granite base made from South Carolina granite. Surmounting the base stood a thirteen-foot bronze palmetto tree. The state's coat of arms graced the upper portion of the base. Two bronze figures representing the only two arms of service from the state kept watch on both sides of the memorial. The monument stood thirty-three feet high. The committee submitted its design to the park commission for approval, and the park historian recommended accepting the proposal if the state removed the battle flag from the face. The South Carolina men agreed.

With the monument nearing completion, the monument committee began preparing for a dedication ceremony. It originally selected July 1901. This would coincide with a Confederate veterans reunion in Memphis. The committee hoped that this date would allow the old soldiers to attend the reunion and stop at the battlefield for the dedication on their return trip home. It would also allow them to take advantage of the low railway rates. Deciding that the July date would not work, the committee selected May 27, 1901, for the ceremony.

Original South Carolina monument. Due to structural problems, the state commission removed the palmetto tree and replaced it with the obelisk. *Courtesy of Chickamauga and Chattanooga National Military Park.*

The park commissioners set up a stage for the distinguished officials and guests. They decorated the platform with the battle flags of the Seventh, Tenth and Twenty-fourth regiments and the United Confederate Veteran camps. On dedication day, the veterans along with the state troops, the governor, state commissioners and park commissioners formed a processional at Lytle Station to march to the monument. The old soldiers, following their battle flags, swelled with pride as onlookers saluted the men as they passed. Arriving at the memorial, the crowd found seats and listened to the prayer offered by General J.B. Kershaw's son. After several rousing speeches remembering the heroism of the Palmetto State soldiers, four young women, selected to represent the four South Carolina commanders, unveiled the monument. The crowd applauded and cheered. It had never seen a more beautiful or fitting monument to its brave soldiers.

Visitors to the park often posed for photos at the base of the monument. Many took home photos of the majestic palmetto tree waving in the wind. The committee, having completed its work, returned to its usual business, satisfied that it had created a fitting memorial. Unfortunately, in 1902, park engineer Edward Betts wrote in his annual report that the monument had problems. The bronze palmetto leaves were proving too fragile for the winds and storms of Georgia. He reported that some leaves had nearly entirely or partially broken off. He recommended that the park commissioners bring the matter to the attention of the South Carolina Commission and that the state get proposals for removing the tree and sending it back to the foundry. It is unclear if the park commission notified the state after the report.

In 1904, state committee member C.I. Walker inquired as to the condition of the monument. Betts reported that the park had repaired the tree the previous year. At the time, it appeared to be in good condition, but the leaves were structurally weak and in need of strengthening. Betts explained to Walker that the swaying and bending in the wind had caused the leaves to become interlocked and break. After careful thought, the park engineer did not recommend strengthening the tree. He believed that a heavier figure would destroy the artistic effect, yet Betts still suggested replacing the tree with something stronger and heavier and placing the current tree indoors in a protected spot. Walker reconvened his committee. After much discussion, the men agreed to remove the tree. They

Right: The South Carolina monument veiled and awaiting dedication, May 27, 1901. *Courtesy of Chickamauga and Chattanooga National Military Park.*

Below: Veterans, commissioners and family members marched to Dyer Field to dedicate the South Carolina monument on May 27, 1901. *Courtesy of Chickamauga and Chattanooga National Military Park.*

129

proposed replacing the tree with a color bearer holding a gathered flag on a staff. The flag would show that it was Confederate. Boynton must have suggested that the committee rethink its new design, as the park had several monuments with color bearers. The South Carolina men finally settled on replacing the bronze piece with a twenty-five-foot-high obelisk shaft. The park commissioners helped the state committee hire a local contractor to scrap the bronze palmetto tree. By December 1904, the park commission had reported that the South Carolina monument now stood complete with the new shaft and ready for inspection. Despite not having the iconic palmetto tree, the imposing monument commands attention on the knoll in Dyer Field.

North Carolina

If these hills and valleys and streams could speak, they would tell of deeds of gallantry, of heroism, of endurance and of sacrifice that once here exemplified, are now fast growing into mere memories and traditions.
—Senator Stokes of Pennsylvania

Only five regiments from North Carolina served in the Battle of Chickamauga. The men served in the opening of the battle with Bushrod Johnson. Others swept along LaFayette Road, forcing the Federal troops back, and crashed the Union line in Kelly field. The men fought a hard-won battle but took many casualties.

Like many southern states, North Carolina struggled with the money to honor its soldiers. The state did not erect monuments to its brave men until the twentieth century. In July 1905, the State of North Carolina submitted plans to erect three monuments on the battlefield. It requested to erect a memorial to the Thirty-ninth Carolina near the little house mentioned in battle reports by Colonel David Coleman. It also wanted a memorial honoring the Sixty-eighth North Carolina on Snodgrass Hill and another monument to the Thirty-eighth near the point where Bushrod Johnson's troops crossed the Federal line.

Above: North Carolina regimental
monument. *Photo by Jane D. Beal.*

Right: Sketch of the proposed Sixtieth
North Carolina regimental monument.
*Courtesy of Chickamauga and Chattanooga
National Military Park.*

One month earlier, the Asheville chapter of the United
Daughters of the Confederacy sent the park commission plans
for a monument to the Sixtieth North Carolina. The men who
served in the regiment had been residents of Asheville and the
surrounding communities. The women proposed erecting the
memorial in Kelly Field and requested the monument be of white
Georgia marble and stand six feet high. The women requested
the stone be inscribed with the inscription, "By the Ashville
Chapter of the Daughters of the Confederacy and friends this
monument is erected. This twentieth day of September 1905.
The forty-second anniversary of this battle. Marking the spot

The Sixtieth North Carolina regimental monument at Chickamauga. *Photo by Jane D. Beal.*

reached by the Sixtieth regiment of North Carolina Volunteers in its charge at noon September 20, 1863. As fixed by the North Carolina state commissioners." Added to the monument would be a list of the regiment's officers and staff.

The park commissioners reviewed the monument design and inscription. The men appeared to have no issue with either one. When reviewing the location of the monument, the commission decided that to be historically accurate, the memorial had to be moved back one hundred yards in the field. Three weeks earlier, the women had measured off the site and marked the location of their monument on the field. The ladies were disheartened and upset. A representative of the chapter wrote in frustration to a park commissioner that they felt their "claims have been unfairly and unjustly treated and respectfully ask to withdraw all papers and propositions looking to the erection of a monument or marker to the Sixtieth regiment." Not all the commissioners agreed with the decision on the monument's location. Alexander P. Stewart wrote to the women that they were correct. He was with the North Carolina commissioners in 1893 when they agreed on the regiment's position. Stewart argued that the site selected by the women was appropriate. Unfortunately, he did not get to make the final decision. In 1905, discouraged and even a bit angry, the women took the money they raised and erected the memorial near the Boscum County Courthouse in Asheville, North Carolina.

Only two regiments received monuments from the State of North Carolina. It is unclear if the state or the veterans themselves paid for the memorials. In November 1905, during a southern immigration quarantine convention in Chattanooga, seven southern governors and Pennsylvania governor Samuel Pennypacker attended. The men traveled out to the battlefield to review the recently erected monuments. The governor of North Carolina joined the state's commission on the battlefield to dedicate the monuments. The ceremony was informal and involved few if any of the state's veterans.

Alabama and Florida

Ah, but who has language to portray the heroism of such brave
souls? They stood by their colors unflinchingly, when carnage,
ruin and death reigned supreme.
            —Alabama governor William C. Oates

The people of Alabama suffered greatly throughout the Civil
War. The opposing armies waged battles across its landscape
and brought hardships on its citizens. The state supplied the
Confederacy with 100,000 soldiers. Despite having seceded and
joined the South, Alabama also provided 6,000 men for the
Union cause. More people fought in the war than could vote. As
a result, the state sacrificed many of its young men in battle. The
women who nervously waited at home and mourned the losses
would not forget the war. They would not forget the sacrifices
made by their loved ones.

Like many southern states, Alabama did not erect monuments
on the battlefield. Despite the involvement of its soldiers and
the Southern victory at Chickamauga, the state never followed
through with erecting a memorial. The women of Alabama
would correct this oversight. In 1913, the Ladies Aid Memorial
Association of Montgomery began the work of erecting a
monument to the soldiers of Alabama. This would not be their
only memorial. Shortly after the war, ladies' aid societies formed
throughout the state to assist in burying the dead soldiers. The
women also advocated and began observing a Confederate
memorial day. As time passed, the association became involved
in assisting the Alabama veterans with building the Confederate
monument in Montgomery. The women realized that the
battlefields preserved by the government lacked memorials to
the Alabama soldiers. The women became determined to rectify
the situation.

In 1907, the Alabama legislature appropriated funds to build
memorials on the battlefields but, for some reason failed to
follow through with making the money available. Determined
to honor their soldiers, the Ladies Memorial Association of

Alabama state monument. *Photo by Jane D. Beal.*

Florida state monument. *Photo by Jane D. Beal.*

Montgomery raised the funds to erect a monument on the Chickamauga battlefield. The women earned $25,000 and selected a design created by Miss Toca Cozart, a member of the association. Cozart was born in Atlanta, Georgia, to a prominent family. Her father, a merchant in the city, died while she was an infant and her grandfather was a founder of the city. The artist's talent came from her mother's side of the family, and they proudly claimed the famed artist Mary Cossat as a relative. The association approached Mr. E.C. Rammage, the son of a Confederate veteran, to help construct the memorial. Rammage, proud of the opportunity to honor the veterans, refused to accept pay. He told the women that the project was a labor of love. On May 28, 1913, during the United Confederate Veteran reunion in Chattanooga, the women dedicated the marble monument to the soldiers of Alabama.

Florida dedicated its monument the same day as the women of Alabama. Like many southern states, Florida also waited to build a monument to its sons. In 1895, the state legislature discussed erecting a monument, but the bill never passed. In 1913, the Florida representatives appropriated $15,000 for a memorial. The state's commissioners selected a design created by the McNeel Marble Works of Marietta, Georgia. The monument featured a granite dome supported by twelve columns and featured a symbolic statue of a soldier at parade rest created by the company's sculptor, L. Milinn. The figure would reside underneath the canopy and the

Florida Commission officially named the Mount Airy granite memorial the *Florida State Soldier's Monument*. In May 1913, during the Confederate veterans reunion, the state dedicated the memorial.

Texas

From this it will be seen that the Southern states have fallen behind Northern states in remembering the valor and patriotism of their sons on these memorable fields.
— *Chickamauga Park Commissioner Baxter Smith*

After the dedication of the Alabama and Florida monuments, it would be a long time before the park would hold another one. The old veterans would long be gone. Many of their children would be very aged or gone. It would take a new generation, one that never fought in the war, to remember the Texas troops.

As the first park commissioners died, a new generation took over the custodianship of the park. The new commissioners noted that most southern states had not built monuments honoring their troops on the battlefield. Park commissioner Baxter Smith began writing to the southern state governors encouraging them to memorialize their sons. Most of the governors made shallow promises to look into the matter or simply did not respond. In 1910, Smith spearheaded efforts to erect a monument to the Texans. After

Texas state monument. *Photo by Jane D. Beal.*

corresponding with state representatives in Texas, he drew up proceedings and a draft of enacting legislation for presentation in the state legislature. Unfortunately, none of the Texas congressmen presented the bill. The number of Texas veterans still living became smaller every year.

Determined to remember the Texans at Chickamauga, the Blue and Gray Association petitioned the governor to make suitable appropriations for a memorial. The frail and elderly soldiers' pleas fell on deaf ears. The Texas chapter of the United Confederate Veterans (UCV) decided to enlist the aid of the Texas citizens and began urging voters to elect candidates who supported building monuments. After the elections, the UCV requested Smith to speak to the state legislature and make an impassioned plea for legislation for a monument. Unable to travel to Austin, the commissioner wrote to the members of the Texas legislature, urging them to remember their sons before they all passed away. The efforts failed, and the old Texas soldiers left the world never seeing a monument on the battlefield in their honor.

In 1961, the United States began a four-year celebration of the 100th anniversary of the Civil War. States held reenactments, and new battlefields were preserved and marked. States quickly began publishing accounts of their troops' involvement. Texas formed a centennial commission to coordinate celebratory activities. The commissioners quickly became aware that Texans lacked memorials on most of the battlefield parks. The centennial commission, using state appropriations, corrected the oversight. Working with the National Park Service staff, the Texans selected the site where General James Deshler's brigade assaulted the Union line on September 20, 1863. It would also be near Deshler's mortuary monument. In April 1963, taking the suggestion of the park staff, the state commission erected the monument. Although it would come one hundred years after the battle, the Texas soldiers finally had a memorial.

Bushrod Johnson Monument

*The world erected monuments in honor of heroic deeds, of
patriotic sacrifice, and of great achievements. It does this, not as
a solace for the dead, but as an inspiration for the living.*
—Illinois governor John P. Altgeld

Bushrod Johnson, who was born in Ohio, led his troops into
some of the fiercest fighting of the battle. The brigadier general
led the Confederate troops in the opening advance of the Battle
of Chickamauga and pressed on Union General Thomas's men
along Horseshoe Ridge. The Confederate general also served
in the Seminole War and the Mexican-American War after
graduating from the United States Military Academy. In 1861,
he left his teaching job to offer his services to the Confederacy.
Johnson's men loved and revered him. After the war, the former
commander became a chancellor at the University of Nashville.
Upon retiring, he moved to Illinois to farm and never returned
alive to the South.

During the mid-1970s, an Illinois Civil War enthusiast named
Noble Wyatt became interested in the Confederate general
buried in Illinois. After much researching, Wyatt discovered
that Johnson's beloved wife lay in rest at the old city cemetery
in Nashville. Believing that Johnson and his wife, Mary, should
be at rest together, Wyatt began the task of having Johnson's
body relocated to Tennessee. After contacting the general's
descendants, the Illinois native reinterred Johnson in Nashville
next to his beloved wife. A scholar of Johnson's Civil War record,
Wyatt decided that the general needed recognition for his
leadership at Chickamauga.

Noble Wyatt worked with the National Park Service to build
a monument in honor of Bushrod Johnson on the battlefield. It
would be one of the few not erected by the veterans themselves.
It would also be one of the few erected in honor of a single
commander by an individual. Wyatt worked at raising funds for
the project. He managed to secure donations from his employer,
Owens-Illinois Glass in Alton, Illinois, as well as from the St. Louis

and Illinois chapters of the Sons of the Confederate Veterans and the United Daughters of the Confederacy. After securing $5,027 in donations, Wyatt hired sculptor Joe Wannamaker of Godfrey, Illinois, to create a bust of the general for the monument.

In September 1977, Wyatt and nine volunteers traveled to the battlefield to build the memorial. With the help of mason Hugh Tieman, the crew constructed the monument on site. On the back, the men set the footstone from Johnson's original grave into the memorial. As the crew completed the stonework, they stopped and signed a certificate to record the names of those working on the project. The men placed the paper in a capsule and set it inside the monument.

Monument to Confederate Brigadier General Bushrod Johnson.

On September 18, 1977, Wyatt and the volunteers, family members, park service personnel and other interested parties gathered at the park to dedicate the monument to Bushrod Johnson. The band from Gordon Lee High School performed the music. The park superintendent, representatives of the Tennessee Historical Commission and the lieutenant governor of Georgia presented speeches in honor of the commander and the efforts of one man to memorialize him. Members of the Sons of Confederate Veterans and the United Daughters of the Confederacy paid their respects to the revered Southern general. Long after they were gone, Americans still remembered and honored the soldiers of the blue and gray.

Epilogue

About 150 years ago, two great armies collided, leaving death and destruction in their wake. The participants would never forget those fateful days. They had been young, and as time passed, they realized the significance of those battles. Years later, the very men who had fought one another gathered on the same fields. They met not to exchange shots but to shake hands and to memorialize the courage and losses. The old soldiers gathered numerous times after the creation of the park to dedicate the various memorials. Men of both sides honored one another at the ceremonies and often wondered aloud whether future Americans would understand or even remember them.

Today, 500,000 people visit the battlefield each year. They hike the trails and snap pictures of the wildlife. A few stop to read the inscriptions on the monuments and take a photo. One has to wonder if most visitors notice the monuments or understand their meaning. It is common on a nice afternoon to see a mother and son playing catch near the Georgia monument or to see college students tossing a Frisbee in an open field. Park visitors seem to miss the soldiers' stories. Vandals have damaged some of the veterans' beloved memorials. Today, many monuments are missing pieces. A granite soldier works to load a missing musket, and the stone commander

Two women pose for a photo in front of the Second Minnesota monument.
Courtesy of Hamilton County Library.

on Snodgrass Hill gestures with arms missing their hands. A cavalryman works to raise a missing sword. During the 1980s, the National Park Service began studying and developing practices for cleaning and preserving the monuments on the battlefields, thus creating a preservation plan. Today, patience and skill combat the damage created by time, the environment and vandals.

It will take more than time, patience and skill to ensure that the monuments remain. Visitors must stop and notice the stones. They must learn to appreciate the efforts that the states put into honoring their sons. The memorials are testaments to the soldiers. They tell of their courage and determination. They are more than nuisances dotting the battlefield. The monuments are the veterans' attempts to keep their stories alive through the ages. One only has to look at the determination on the face of the Tennessee cavalryman raising his sword in battle or in the eyes of the wounded soldier on the Second Minnesota monument to understand the sadness, pride and love of the old soldiers. As a visitor, stop and read the inscriptions and admire the artwork. Listen carefully because the soldiers are telling you their story of the battle.

SELECTED BIBLIOGRAPHY

PRIMARY SOURCES

Belknap, Charles E. *History of Michigan Organizations at Chickamauga-Chattanooga and Missionary Ridge.* Lansing, MI.: Robert Smith Printing Company, 1899.

Boynton, Henry V. *Chattanooga and Chickamauga: Reprint of General H.V. Boynton's Letters to the Cincinnati Gazette, August 1888.* Project Gutenberg e-book, Library of Alexandria, 2011.

————. *The National Military Park, Chickamauga-Chattanooga.* Cincinnati, OH: Robert Clark Company, 1895.

"Ceremonies at the Unveiling of the South Carolina Monument Chickamauga Battlefield, May 27, 1901." Chickamauga archives, n.d.

Chickamauga and Chattanooga National Military Park, War Department Commission Files. Series II, Accession No. 205. Chickamauga, Georgia.

Chickamauga Memorial Association. *Proceedings at Chattanooga, Tennessee and Crawfish Springs, Georgia, September 19 and 20, 1889.* N.p.: Chattanooga Army of the Cumberland Reunion Entertainment Committee, 1889.

Clark, Charles T. *Opdycke Tigers, 125th OVI: A History of the Regiment and the Campaigns and Battles of the Army of the Cumberland.* Columbus, OH: Spahn and Glenn, 1895.

Cory, Marielou Armstrong. *The Ladies Memorial Association of Montgomery.* Montgomery, AL: Montgomery Printing Company, 1902.

Georgia Commission. *Report of the Georgia State Memorial Board on the Monuments and Markers Erected on the Chickamauga Battlefield.* Atlanta, GA: Franklin Printing and Publishing Company, 1899.

Indiana at Chickamauga: Report of the Indiana Commission Chickamauga National Military Park. Indianapolis, IN: William B. Buford, 1901.

Judson Wade Bishop and Family Papers. Minnesota Historical Society, P1922 Box 2.

Kentucky Board of Commissioners. *Kentucky State Monuments and Markers.* N.p., n.d.

Kilborn, L.S. *Dedication of the Wilder Brigade Monument on the Chickamauga Battlefield on the Thirty-sixth Anniversary of the Battle, September 29, 1894.* Marshall, IL: Herald Press, 1900.

Kingman, Leroy W. *Instructions of the New York Board of Commissioners for the Monuments at the Battlefields of Chattanooga.* N.p., n.d.

McElroy, Joseph C. *Chickamauga: Record of the Ohio Chickamauga and Chattanooga National Park by the Ohio Chickamauga-Chattanooga National Park Commission.* Cincinnati, OH: Earhardt and Richardson, 1896.

Oates, William B. *Speech of Governor William B. Oates of Alabama Delivered at Chattanooga, Tennessee, September 20, 1895, on the Battles of Chickamauga and Chattanooga*. Montgomery, AL: Boemer Printing, 1895.

Porter, Joseph D. *Tennessee State Monuments and Markers: Report of the Commission*. Nashville, TN: Foster and Webb, 1898.

Report of the Minnesota Commissioners to Locate the Positions and Erect Monuments on the Battlefields of Chickamauga and Chattanooga and of the Dedications of Said Monuments. N.p., n.d.

Sherman, Ernest A. *Dedicating in Dixie*. Cedar Rapids, IA: Record Printing Company, 1907.

Skinner, George W., ed. *Pennsylvania at Chickamauga and Chattanooga: Ceremonies and Dedication of Monuments*. N.p., 1897.

Sutherland, G. Frank. *Report of the New Jersey Chickamauga-Chattanooga Park Commission to Excellency, Honorable John W. Griggs Governor*. Somerville, NJ: Unionist Gazette Print, 1897.

Taylor, Benjamin F. Scrapbook. Colonel Benjamin Franklin Taylor Collection, MS 1863, Box 2, Scrapbook 5. Maryland Historical Society library, Baltimore, Maryland.

Twentieth Iowa Official Register. Published by the Iowa Secretary of State, 1905.

Twenty-first Iowa Official Register. Published by the Iowa Secretary of State, 1905.

SECONDARY SOURCES

Chaffee, Linda Smith, John B. Coduri and Ellen L. Madison. *Built from Stone: The Westerly Granite Story*. Westerly, RI: Babcock Smith House, 2011.

Clark, Rod. *Carved in Stone: A History of the Barre Granite Industry*. Barre, VT: Rock of Ages Corporation, 1989.

Cozzens, Peter. *The Battle of Chickamauga: The Terrible Sound*. Urbana: University of Illinois Press, 1992.

———. *The Battles for Chattanooga: The Shipwreck of Their Hopes*. Urbana: University of Illinois Press, 1994.

Davis, Steve. *Johnny Reb in Perspective: The Confederate Soldier's Image in the Southern Arts*. Atlanta, GA: Emory University, 1979.

Elliott, Sam Davis. *Soldier of Tennessee: General Alexander P. Stewart and the Civil War in the West*. Baton Rouge: Louisiana State University, 1999.

Garvey, Timothy J. *Public Sculptor: Lorado Taft and the Beautification of Chicago*. Urbana: University of Illinois, 1988.

Hallmark, Richard Parker. "Chicago Sculptor Richard W. Bock: Social and Artistic Demands at the Turn of the Twentieth Century." PhD diss., St. Louis University, 1980.

Illinois State Historical Society. Papers in "Illinois History and Transactions for the Year 1941." Springfield: Illinois State Historical Society, 1943.

Lowe, William C. "A Grand and Patriotic Pilgrimage: The Iowa Civil War Monuments Dedication Tour of 1906." *Annals of Iowa* 69, no. 1 (Winter 2010): 1–50.

Marten, James. *Sing Not War: The Lives of Union and Confederate Veterans During the Gilded Age*. Chapel Hill: University of North Carolina, 2011.

McCullough, David. *The Greater Journey: Americans in Paris*. New York: Simon and Schuster, 2011.

McDonough, James Lee. *Chattanooga: A Death Grip on the Confederacy*. Knoxville: University of Tennessee, 1984.

Nonestied, Mark, and Richard Veit. "Some Beautiful Monuments I've Made: Identifying Nineteenth and Twentieth Century Monument Makers," December 2011. Garden State Legacy. www.gardenstatelegacy.com.

Paige, John C. *Administrative History of Chickamauga and Chattanooga National Military Park*. Denver, CO: National Park Service, 1983.

Pierre, Dorathai Bock, ed. *Memoirs of an American Artist: Sculptor Richard W. Bock*. Los Angeles, CA: C.C. Publishing, 1989.

Robertson, William Glenn. "The Chickamauga Campaign." *Blue and Gray* 24, no. 3 (Fall 2007): 6–59.

Sessions, Eugene, ed. *Celebrating a Century of Granite Art*. N.p., n.d.

Smith, Timothy B. *A Chickamauga Memorial: The Establishment of America's First National Military Park*. Knoxville: University of Tennessee, 2009.

———. *The Golden Age of Preservation*. Knoxville: University of Tennessee, 2008.

Taft, Ada Bartlett. *Lorado Taft Sculptor and Citizen*. N.p.: Mary Taft Smith, 1947.

Taft, Lorado. *Famous American Sculptors*. Ann Arbor: University of Michigan, 1903.

———. *The History of American Sculpture*. N.p.: Forgotten Books, 2012.

NEWSPAPERS

Baltimore Sun.

Chattanooga Free Press.

Chattanooga Times.

Hartford Courant.

New York Times.

INDEX

About the Author

Dr. Stacy Reaves received her PhD from Oklahoma State University and is currently an adjunct professor of history and geography at Tulsa Community College. With a bachelor's degree in historic preservation from Southeast Missouri State University, she has served as a museum director at Sand Springs Cultural and Historical Museum and as curator at Sapulpa Historical Society and the Fort Sill Army Museum. She has worked as a seasonal interpretative park ranger at Shiloh National Military Park for five years. Dr. Reaves's writings have appeared in the *Chronicles of Oklahoma*, *North and South* magazine, the *Journal of the West* and the *Journal of Military History*. Dr. Reaves also wrote *A History and Guide to the Monuments of Shiloh National Park*.

ALSO BY THIS AUTHOR

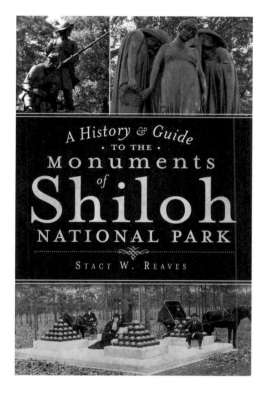

978.1.60949.412.4 * 5.5 x 8.5 * 128 PP * $17.99
PUBLISHED JANUARY 2012

The events of the Battle of Shiloh are characterized by acts of bravery, sacrifice and uncommon valor. Established just over three decades after the battle ended, Shiloh National Park gave veteran groups from states across the country an opportunity to memorialize their regiments' specific contributions. Each monument, like the soldiers themselves, has a story to tell. *A History & Guide to the Monuments of Shiloh National Park* recounts the history of the park's creation and the monuments' construction. Join former Shiloh National Park interpreter and seasonal guide Stacy W. Reaves as she charts the paths through the park's grounds and traces its fascinating history.

Visit us at
www.historypress.net
··
This title is also available as an e-book